Kalât Claimed

A play

by

Bahram Beyzaie

Translated by

Manuchehr Anvar

Bisheh Publishing – San Francisco, USA

Kalât Claimed

A Play by Bahram Beyzaie

Translated by Manuchehr Anvar

Written in : 1982
Translated in : 1997
Cover Design : Mohsen Valihi

Copyright 2022 by Bahram Beyzaie
All rights reserved, including the right to reproduce this book
or portion thereof in any form whatsoever.

Library of Congress Control Number: 2022933267
ISBN: 978-1-7355686-5-2

The publication of this book was made possible by the Hamid
and Christina Moghadam Program in Iranian Studies at
Stanford University.

Bisheh Publishing – San Francisco, USA
Bisheh.publishing@gmail.com
www.bisheh-publishing.com
Published in the United States of America

Kalât
Claimed

Characters

Tuy Khân *Aralât*
Gur Khân *Suldus*
Qarâ Khân *Oyerât*
Qâidu *Ur Khân*
Vatvât *Nâymân*
Yâmât *Tuqâi Khân*
Dinkiz *Bâyâvot*
Qanqrât *Qârât Khân*
Inânj *Yulduz*
Qâii Bâyât

Ây Bânu
Attendant 1
Old Woman 1 *Old Woman 2*
Old Woman 3 *Old Woman 4*
Messenger A

Storyteller *Five Headed Woman*
Attendant 2 *Servants*
Table Decker *Jailer*
Executioner *Messengers 1-6*
Old Pishmarg *Young Pishmarg*
Judges *Whores*
Children *Envoy*
Scribe *Others*

Scene
An empty space

Props
Nets, severed heads, pennants, banners, flags, a spinning wheel, a carriage, a dummy, seven veils of Ây Bânu, arms and armour, etc.

STORYTELLER: Hear, o hear, o hear!
              Lend ear to the old storyteller!
              Hear about hardy desert heroes
              dragon-bodied riders
              and riderless horses.
              About Tuy Khân and Tuqâi Khân
              two lusty warriors
              both fabled.
              Their horses' hooves
              beating boulders into dust.
              Knotty-browed
              steel-veined
              granite-bosomed
              and iron-fisted.
              This one slaying
              no matter whom.
              And that
              breaking every back.
              Two raging cyclones
              the likes of whom

no battlefield did ever sustain.
In the battle of battles
no one knew
which of the two
had the upper hand
and was fiercer in combat.
Both darkly clad
grim and obdurate.
They did not battle
but crumpled steel.
That was the day when warriors
dipped their faces
in their enemies' blood.
The mere mention of their names
would send the enemy
scampering off to the hills.
But where to hide
from the scourge of their arrows?
No one could choose between them
for this one thrived on destruction
and that traded in death.
When Tuy set fire to tents
Tuqâi raped and plundered.
If this one returned with a thousand
bales of loot
the other counted as many heads of
captives.
Now
this is the field of the fallen...
Look well!
Remember those two fabled names:
Tuy Khân and Tuqâi Khân
Tuy, the conqueror of Kalât

Tuqâi, the ruler of Balkh and Bâmiân.
This, The Seven-Headed Commander
The Taker of Souls
and that, The Captive-Killing Khân
The Death-Monger.
Nay.
Where and when
even The Angel of Death himself
in the course of a single day
did make a mountain of corpses
did raise a tower of severed heads
and did fill the desert with groans
and clear it of enemies?

[Sounds of bugle. Moving dust. Tuy Khân, seen in ripped blood-stained armour. Five spears, topped by severed heads, are fastened to his back. With his hands, he carries two more heads, clasping them by the hair.]

STORYTELLER: It is time to look!
This is Tuy Khân:
The Seven-Headed Commander
The Conqueror of Kalât
known as The Taker of Souls.

[Sounds of bugle. Moving dust. Tuqâi Khân appears in armour, covered head to foot with dust and blood. Two wide and long leather straps are tied to his shoulders and attached to a huge net, filled with broken captives, and dragged behind him.]

STORYTELLER: And this, Tuqâi Khân:
The Captive-Killing Khân

                    The Lord of Balkh and Bâmiân
                    known as The Death-Monger.

                    [Sounds of thunder.]

STORYTELLER: This dust is not of storm
                    but of the hooves of horses.
                    This stretch of red earth
                    is not a field of puppies
                    but a desert of fallen warriors.

                    [Sounds of horns.]

TUY KHÂN: *[Counting]*
                    Six rows of ten
                    seven tens
                    eight tens.
                    Nine rows of ten.
                    Ten rows of ten.
                    One row of a hundred!

TUQÂI KHÂN: *[Counting]*
                    This, a second hundred.
                    That makes two hundred!
                    So, I should begin with another row of ten.
                    Another row of ten.
                    The third row of ten.
                    The fourth row of ten...

TUY KHÂN: *[Continues]*
                    Fifth row of ten.
                    Another row again...

BOTH: *[Continuing]*
                    Now the seventh row.

                         This, the eighth row.
                         The ninth row full.
                         The tenth row aside.
                         That makes three hundred!

STORYTELLER: Count, count, count... What?
                         They count...
                         The corpses of the slain!
                         For every row of ten
                         one stroke of the cymbal!
                         For five tens
                         gongs and bells!
                         For each row of a hundred
                         the clamor of horns, bugles
                         and tambourines.
                         The horn, the drum
                         and cries of exultation
                         from the heroes of the rows!

TUY & TUQÂI: *[Counting]*
                         Three rows of a hundred.
                         Three rows of ten.
                         Three more tens.
                         Fully, three hundred and sixty counted!
                         But this last corpse...

TUY KHÂN: I slew him!

TUQÂI KHÂN: I!

TUY KHÂN: Your proof?

TUQÂI KHAN: His smile!

TUY KHÂN: Take it!

TUQÂI KHÂN: Hah! What arrogance!

TUY KHÂN:	His youthful face as it was cleft in two full of horror is still before my eyes.
TUQÂI KHÂN:	Holding a pennant he was cut in two by my sword.
TUY KHÂN:	He cried: "Mother!" And I struck.
TUQÂI KHÂN:	The terror of my mace broke his back.
TUY KHÂN:	You called me a liar!
TUQÂI KHÂN:	You took to denials!
TUY KHÂN:	This corpse is mine!
TUQÂI KHÂN:	Mine!

[Seventeen Commanders have entered from different corners: experienced in war, young and old.]

TUY KHÂN:	Look well at the wound rent by my sword! Who would fail to recognize the double slash that's my hall-mark?
TUQÂI KHÂN:	My arrow of pheasant's plume is still in him right up to the feathery tip. Who would fail to notice it lodged as it is right down to the sixth joint?
TUY KHÂN:	Take note of the slit wrought by my spear!

TUQÂI KHÂN:	And this is the gash that fits my javelin!
TUY KHÂN:	Do not fight with me for a corpse!
TUQÂI KHÂN:	The glory of this battle hangs on the last corpse. Three rows of a hundred six of ten have I slain. And this the counters have counted by the traces of my javelin and my arrows.
TUY KHÂN:	Three rows of a hundred and six of ten I have killed and more —according to the verdict of the judges. Let judges come and decide the case!
TUQÂI KHÂN:	Let experts come: men wise in war. He who killed this one shall reap the glory.
TUY KHÂN:	Speak, experts in the name of King Tongqut Khân our triumphant Sovereign whose flags of victory fly throughout the desert. Speak!

JUDGES: We experts are afraid
for if we tell the truth
or make mistakes
one of the two
Tuy Khân or Tuqâi Khân
shall be vexed.
And so
we too
shall count among the slain.

STORYTELLER: In the name of the Great Tongqut Khân
a book of victory was written
by dignitaries.
The spoils of war
the captives
both divided
in equal parts.
The fury of the two Commanders
also of equal measure.

TUQÂI KHÂN: *[To himself]*
You wish to wrest this corpse from me
as you did Ây Bânu.
Ây Bânu
not your wife
but the woman you robbed me off.
And now you possess her
only because
by trickery
you gained the gates of the City
one single hour
before I did.

TUY KHÂN: *[To judges]*

                          The matter at hand
                          is not a corpse
                          but the glory of the battle.

JUDGES: The Great Khân himself
                          was as loath as we are
                          to set one of you two heroes
                          above the other.

STORYTELLER: Now is the season for feasts of victory
                          time for the lute and the lyre
                          for wine and song.
                          A hundred heads of horses
                          and three hundred sheep.
                          The pleasing aroma of meat grills
                          fills the desert air.
                          Songsters are turning the battle into a
                          song.
                          By turns
                          horns are being blown
                          at the Six Gates.

TUY KHÂN: Chief Commander Tuqâi Khân
                          head to a group of Generals
                          put your fury down!
                          In my dominion
                          The Fortress of Kalât
                          with honour
                          I shall feast you
                          if you let me.
                          And lyrists shall sing
                          the tale of your victory
                          and that of mine
                          from the tops of the fortress' walls.

TUQÂI KHÂN:	Tuy Khân Defeater of Surrounding Sovereigns since you make peace there is no quarrel. I accept this banquet. Enough of war! The host and his men lead the way. The guest and his friends follow.
TUY KHÂN:	*[To himself]* He comes to my palace and I shall make him ashamed with certain feasts! But in the Book of Heroes the name of Tuy Khân shall be placed before that of Tuqâi Khân just as his horse is always and in every battle a full furlong ahead of that of the boastful Tuqâi.
TUQÂI KHÂN:	*[To Qâii Bâyât]* I have reason for attending this banquet. I go, hoping that for a moment at least I may see Ây Bânu the one who is the head among the Turks, the Arabs and the Persians and to whom belongs my heart.
QÂII BÂYÂT:	You should know, Commander

| | that you shall not see Ây Bânu.
| | She's sent to Safe Enclosures
| | up in the mountains.
| | The Summer Quarters
| | the place is called.
| | You shall not see Ây Bânu.

TUQÂI KHÂN: Yet
to avenge what the cursed fellow
has done to me
I shall attend the banquet.
Dinkiz, Inânj, Bâyâvot, Yulduz, Qânqrât,
Qârât Khân
and you, Qâii Bâyât.
You Commanders
shall wield your arms
at the table of their feast
and quench your thirst
by drinking their blood!
Once we capture the Palace
and beat the drum
we shall rule
The Kalâtians.
Qâii Bâyât!
You are the courier
who shall take the message
to Ây Bânu.
And as she returns
from the Summer Quarters
she'll find herself at my Palace.

TUY KHÂN: You Commanders
shall take up your arms at the banquet
and drag their greed for gluttony

                out of their gullets
and dye the dining spread with their
blood!
Gur Khân, Qârâ Khân
Nâymân, Suldus
Arâlât, Oyerât
Ur Khân, Vatvât
Qâidu, Yâmât!
Set hard at them
and make them vomit
their own blood!
There cannot be a better chance.

GUR KHÂN: You're the ruler, Tuy Khân.
I tremble with fear
and obey
though guest-killing
is not to my taste.

DINKIZ: You're the Commander, Tuqâi Khân.
Whatever pleases you
shall be done
though no blessing will attend
the murder of those
whose salt we share.

[Sounds of drums and horns.]

STORYTELLER: They signal:
it is time to set forth.

QÂII BÂYÂT: Pull out the tent-pegs!

STORYTELLER: Raise all flags and pennants!
Tie the enemy's head
to the saddle side!

The red-mantled horse
shall yield to you
Commander!

[Everyone has gone out. The stage is empty. Slowly, the five-headed woman enters. On her shoulders, she carries a long stick, to which hang four heads with long hair and robes, reaching the ground, all dark and tattered.]

FIVE-HEADED WOMAN: We Five Eternal Sisters
exhausted
on foot
helpless.
Four dead
only one living.
Seeking what?
Searching for whom?

[Humming]

The saviour on the gallows.
Overlords thirsting for blood.
Troops perfidious.
People sore of heart.
Our days dull and dim.
Our grief pervasive.
Our state lamentable.
Hooo! Hooo! Hooo!

[Six of Tuy Khân's Commanders enter. Seeing her, they are stunned.]

YÂMÂT: What horrible place is this?

FIVE-HEADED WOMAN: The world.

YÂMÂT: And what're you doing here?

FIVE-HEADED WOMAN: Living.

NÂYMÂN: She looks like the dead.

FIVE-HEADED WOMAN: The world is but a graveyard.

NÂYMÂN: What creature are you?

FIVE-HEADED WOMAN: A living soul
unfamiliar with life
a dead being
searching for a grave.

QÂIDU: Where is she off to?

FIVE-HEADED WOMAN: To the banquet.

QÂIDU: What do they serve at this banquet?

FIVE-HEADED WOMAN: The Commanders' heads.

YÂMÂT: Yes.
The Tuqânians.

ARALÂT: You have four silent companions with you
one of them holding a tattered fan.
The other, an empty flask.
The third, an extinct torch.
And the fourth, a mud-brick.

UR KHÂN: The four elements of life
according to the religion of the Kalâtians.

ARALÂT: And themselves devoid of life.

FIVE-HEADED WOMAN: I bury, bury and bury
past hopes that followed lost days.
I borrow, borrow and borrow
new hopes from tomorrow.

SULDUS: She is an Alân[1], Yâmât.
You should know that.

NÂYMÂN: And we are all
the object of her taunts.

FIVE-HEADED WOMAN: Would that I had never set eyes on you!
Would that your days were numbered!

NÂYMÂN: *[Drawing his sword]*
Silence her!
The Book of Curses she recites.

QÂIDU: Sheath your sword!
Beware of such foul blood!

ARALÂT: She's a babbler.
Let us not listen to her.
Away!
With such a great task ahead of us
we must not tarry.
Let us make haste.
Tuy Khân and his guests
should arrive any time now.
Let us go spread the table!

[Exit Commanders. Woman moves gently around and sits gently down.]

FIVE-HEADED WOMAN: We Five Eternal Sisters
weep for whom?
Moan for what?
I stitch your clothes
o my imagined child.
My heart is sheathed in rust.

---

[1] *An Aryan tribe.*

                  Flowers are so many thorns to me.
                  A mountain of woe
                  is weighing down my heart.
                  Hail to you
                  companions of death!

                  [Tuy Khân, accompanied by four of his Commanders. They are astounded by the sight of the woman.]

TUY KHÂN: Huh!
With such a strange aspect
blocking my way
who are you woman?

FIVE-HEADED WOMAN: I am I
I!

QARA KHÂN: Creation is full of wonders
or perhaps
nothing is more strange
than Creation itself.
Look at her display:
four emblems of life
dead!
And only death itself
is living.

VATVÂT: This is an allusion to us!

FIVE-HEADED WOMAN: I was the sister of a brother
daughter of a father.
Heavens took them away
and the earth devoured them.
Home, shattered.
Husband, dead.

	Child, gone with hope. I was the guardian of the spring you dried.
VATVÂT:	What is the thread and needle for?
UR KHÂN:	She sews something. Unfolds a skein. Stitching—for whom?
FIVE-HEADED WOMAN:	I stitch moments together getting myself dressed with Time patching days with nights. My warps and woofs are worn out. Undone are the seams of my fortune undarned the rents in my soul. With a stack of black hair I weave a mantle of mourning. And to fashion your shrouds I turn my hair into cotton.
GUR KHÂN:	You sinister apparition! *[Drawing his sword]* Talking of death?
VATVÂT:	*[Stops him]* For the ennemy!
TUY KHÂN:	Hum! What fantasies have you clothed us in? Why do you sit in our way? You are both human and fairy-like.

| | There's the power of a talisman in
your lament.
Do you know
there's a feast
in Kalât? |
|---|---|
| FIVE-HEADED WOMAN: | Everyone shall be given their dues
—yes.
Ours
our briny tears. |
| TUY KHÂN: | Why tears
while I scatter gladness?
Let Shamans chant their incantations
to ward off calamity!
When Kalât sits down to its feast
cast a piece of bone to her
to shield us from her inauspiciousness! |
| QARA KHÂN: | Your bidding shall be done, Tuy Khân.
Let us go
for guests are arriving.
You're late.
Let us make haste! |

[They go. The Five-Headed woman, tearing at her hair, moans.]

FIVE-HEADED WOMAN: Five Eternal Sisters that we are
whom should we hail?
To whom should we bid farewell?
Beware of this traveller-on-foot!
Heed that horseman!
As the bird of regret
I lament

                    Woe, woe, woe!
                    As the owl of exile
                    I wail, wail and wail.
                    I am a broken-winged wretch.
                    Woe is me!
                    As a bedraggled crow
                    I caw, caw and caw.

                    [Enter Tuqâi Khân and his seven Commanders.]

QÂRÂT KHÂN: What is this... phantom
                    without a tongue for salutation
                    or welcome
                    with her back
                    to respect and reverence?
                    A word of greeting, dog!

FIVE-HEADED WOMAN: Hail
                    fearsome conquerors!
                    Welcome
                    torch-bearers of destruction!

TUQAI KHÂN: What is this
                    a shadow?
                    Or the shadow of a shadow?
                    It may be the spirit of a tree
                    or a waterhole.
                    The sight of this fairy
                    congeals the blood in my veins!
                    Did I ever burn a tree
                    or cause a waterhole to dry?

COMMANDERS: *[Circling around him]*
                    No, you did not.

	You did not, Commander!
DINKIZ:	Come, Commander! She's neither a phantom nor a fairy.

[To woman.]

Long-tongued babbler!
Who are you
sitting in the dust of the road?
I've seen you yesterday
and the day before.

FIVE-HEADED WOMAN: I'm a mirror to you all!

DINKIZ: What fabrication is this, fiend?
For you're surely no more
than an easy whore!

FIVE-HEADED WOMAN: How can your mirror be
but broken?
In me
you have each spent a time
and passed on
throwing only stones at me.
And I still lie in the dust
and dust is settled on me.
O for a hand
to sweep away this dust
and make me shine!
To lift the rust
from my broken heart
and make me glow with fire
once again
and thus

	cleanse me of you all.
BÂYÂVOT:	Ugly woman! Leprosy is upon you leprosy and small-pox!
FIVE-HEADED WOMAN:	Look at your own ugliness! In me behold your triumph and its crop of pain and destruction!
TUQAI KHÂN:	Aim at her from every side! Put arrows into her from far away!

[Woman moaning.]

DINKIZ:	Hold back Commander! They have killed her yesterday and the day before!

[Woman moaning.]

INÂNJ:	If you look well you shall see arrows already lodged in her.

[Woman moaning.]

YULDUZ:	What with the wounds from arrows in your flesh?

[Woman moaning.]

QANQRÂT:	Die woman

	die in pain and terror!
FIVE-HEADED WOMAN:	Watch your own death in me
in pain and terror!
You conquerors shall all perish.
QÂII BÂYÂT:	Catch her...
The other side...
Cast the rope...
Again...
From every side!
QÂRÂT KHÂN:	She vanished
laughing.
BÂYÂVOT:	This is a trick
spawned by your fancy.
INÂNJ:	Is she truly dead, Commanders?
TUQAI KHÂN:	Do not ask!
Men ought not to think
of sorcerers and women.
Away!
Do not look back
or you'll be haunted
by her blood!
QÂII BÂYÂT:	I hear the sound of their horns.
They come to meet us.
TUQAI KHÂN:	Away!
Trays are spread
and our appetite
for the table laid in Kalât
is sharper than that of our hosts.

[They go.]

STORYTELLER: Out of all the birds
only two have been spared:
the carrier pigeon
and the preying hawk.
The rest are all laid on the tray
well cooked
and seasoned with spices.
The air of Kalât is filled
with the scent of grilling game.
Chunks of meat
in abundance
everywhere.
Joints of buffaloes
zebras
and horses' flesh.
Francolins
gazelles
partridges
calves and lambs.
all eyes in Kalât
are fixed on this banquet.

[Ur Khân passes through.]

UR KHÂN: Bring Bagmaz[1], Qâvout[2] and honey
Qeymeh,[3] Qormeh,[4] Qeymâq[5] and Cheqertmeh[6]!
Fetch the grills!

---

[1] *Large bowl of wine.*
[2] *A compound of pulverized roasted peas, sugar and spices.*
[3] *Chopped meat with cereals.*
[4] *Preserved lamb stew.*
[5] *Clotted cream.*
[6] *Fried minced meat with vegetables.*

| | Come Khân!
| | Your guests
| | are in the eating room.
| | It should not be said
| | that you keep your guests waiting.

TUY KHÂN: If we stop their mouths
it never will.
Fetch an ink-pot, Qarâ Khân.
Have a letter dispatched
to the mighty Tongqut Khân
and let him know
that the foul-blooded Tuqâi
and his Generals
—the villainous plotters—
had set out to pounce
on the renowned City of Kalât
and to replace the dread name of the
mighty Khân
in the daily homage
with that of the treacherous Tuqâi
—may the Devil erase his name!
Thus
they have broken their covenant
with a sovereign
in whose name
I tend this region of Khotalân and Kalât.
That is what you must write!
We should then wait to receive
rich bounties and fresh titles
from His Highness.
Say we would have dispatched the
traitors

yoked and manacled.
But since they drew swords
they were
per force
slain by swords.
That is all.

[Exit Qara Khân. Aralât has already entered.]

Well Aralât
should we not go to the eating room?
Are they all ready?

ARALÂT: My Liege, Tuy Khân, think!
The quarrel is about a single corpse
against which
you're about to make
many new ones.
Why not overcome enmity
with the armor of friendship
lest they call you "Guest-Killer"?
Heed my good counsel
or dispatch a messenger
to ask for Ây Bânu's advice
before it's too late!

TUY KHÂN: I know what passes through your mind.
"Killer-of-Foes" is my title.
And now the foes are at my table.
Ây Bânu is but a woman
and as such
unfit to judge the deeds of men.
You think her wise
and that she truly is.

But what fascinates you
is her beauty
not her wisdom.
Go
attend to the guests now
and soak them in wine!
I shall arrive after the gifts.

[Exit Aralât.]

Ay, there are gifts:
lethal cups
and swords
tempered with poison.

[Cries out.]

Come, Robe-Master
and fetch me the crimson habit
that drapes me
at times of victory!

*[The Robe-Master passes the scene quickly.
Tuy Khân closes his eyes.]*

Ah Tuqâi
listen to the fiddles
specially tuned for you
and the sinister melody
sung in your name.
Drink from the flask
filled with poison
and let a mud-brick
be your pillow!

>   Now
>   you're the very corpse
>   you thought was yours!

TUQAI KHÂN: No!

[Tuy Khân, opening his eyes, finds himself surrounded by Tuqâi's Generals. A quick, terrified reaction by Tuy Khân. But it is too late. Generals, each draw two swords with both hands. They grab Tuy Khân by his sleeves, his riding boots, the back and the sides of his girdle, and his shoulders. Tuy Khân is trapped in their midst.]

> That corpse is none but you, Tuy Khân!
> I well detected the snare
> behind your kindness
> in which you yourself
> are now trapped.

[He waves a letter.]

> In the letter to His Highness
> let it be said that he plotted
> to soil the daily homage
> to His Highness in Kalât
> with his accursed name.
> Being your devoted servant
> our struggle to contain him
> sprang from our duty.
> The rebellion was quelled
> and he is now in chains.

[Tuy Khân is put in chains and fetters. He tries to seize a sword.]

But since he has reached
for the trenchant sword
he shall needs be felled
by the same trenchant sword.
Dinkiz, Qanqrât
tell men
to let the soldiers of Tuy Khân know
that they should give up their swords
and put down their javelins!
Let them beware
of being obstinate
for their Head
has his feet in fetters
and his neck in halters.
Give me his seal!
Now
this Firmân with this seal
for those who recognize
neither the drum-beats of amnesty
nor the bugle-sounds of surrender!

[Commander Qâidu, distraught, enters.]

QÂIDU: Khân, Khân!
Table-deckers are all dead.
Do something!
The archers are in your Palace!

[Everyone turns to him. He is jolted. Wondering.]

The missing guests are here!

[Shouts.]

	Host killers!
TUQAI KHÂN:	Your name is Qâidu. I know what passes through your head. Surrender your sword!
BÂYÂVOT:	Your hands are tied and his blood is held in pledge. Seasoned soldier that you are familiar with vicissitudes of war do not miss your chance!
YULDUZ:	You ride a beleaguered horse and you have dust in your eyes. Yield or you'll be responsible for the shedding of much blood!
QÂIDU:	What if I escape? Tuy Khân You are the Commander; Tell me!
TUY KHÂN:	*[Through clenched teeth]* Go! Run!
QÂIDU:	*[Draws sword]* Who's there?

[As everyone turns around, he disappears.]

TUQAI KHÂN:	Ohoy, pass the word! Beat the alarm! One of them slipped through the net.

[Swords drawn, Bâyâvot and Yulduz run after Qâidu, as Qâii Bâyât, distraught, enters.]

QÂII BÂYÂT: What shall I say, my Liege?
At the slightest suspicion
Tuy Khân's Commanders
one by one
bolted like nimble ghosts
each in a different direction.

QANQRÂT: What if they warn Tuy Khân's units?

DINKIZ: And disappear among the crowds?

INÂNJ: Once disguised
They shall be lost to our sight.

TUQAI KHÂN: Why do you stand still?
Beat the alarm!
Before mice hide in their holes
lay traps in their way!

[Qâii Bâyât and Inânj, swords drawn, have already gone out. Qânqrât and Qârât Khân, pressing their lances on Tuy Khân's shoulders, force him to kneel as he struggles to resist them.]

TUY KHÂN: No Tuqâi!
They know Kalât better than you
this city of enclosures within enclosures
this jammed lock!

[The four Commanders who had just gone out, return, crest-fallen.]

TUQAI KHÂN: Now
close the Six Gates all

and search those who leave or enter
until this ruffian
meets his end.
Go
quick
about your tasks!

[The four Commanders run out in different directions. Tuqâi yells.]

Now, let the dining spread be brought in
I am hungry!

[The table-decker passes through the stage.]

Sit, Tuy Khân!
They shall now fetch the cleaver
the leather spread
the apron
and the basin[1].
We shall soon call
the Jailer and the Executioner.
Now kneel down
and learn to be courteous!
If you have a God
call for His help
or even ask the Angel of Death
to make your exit easy.

TUY KHÂN: I have never asked
              for an easy death.

TUQAI KHÂN: You tussled with me over a corpse.

---

[1] *Cleaver, leather spread, apron and basin are among tools for beheading a condemned man.*

	You're a corpse yourself now, Tuy Khân! You wanted to take away from me the honor that like a corpse lay before my very feet; thinking it, too to be Ây Bânu?
TUY KHÂN:	What did you say about Ây Bânu?
TUQAI KHÂN:	You wanted the lyricists to sing the praise of your victory. Yes let them sing... but the praise of your wife!
TUY KHÂN:	What do you mean, knave?
TUQAI KHÂN:	No one asked Ây Bânu whom she would take for a husband. She went to the nuptial pavillion on her father's command. It was her fate to belong like a war booty to him who had killed more.
TUY KHÂN:	We're both warriors, Tuqâi not a pair of rascals!
TUQAI KHÂN:	You from Khotalân and I from Bâmiân both equal in rank came to the region of Khâvarân on Tangqut Khân's command. You took her

| | because you arrived sooner
entrenching yourself
on a patch of elevated ground. |
|---|---|
| TUY KHÂN: | I won the battle Tuqâi
everyone knows that. |
| TUQAI KHÂN: | It wasn't Ây Bânuyou wanted.
You craved union
with her father's dominion
the kingdom that lies
between the Black River
and the River Alân
with an extent
Equal to seven dawns and sunsets
if covered by a wakeful horseman
on a tireless mount
galloping through the expanse
the land of Yorts and Obbehs[1]
pastures teeming with animals
black tents
wooded hunting grounds and hillocks
villages and townships
with enclosures and battlements
with this city of Kalât
as its beating heart
—this land of Alân warriors. |
| TUY KHÂN: | We tripped them all.
We made the warriors yield
and set fire to their black tents.
In the end
they had no choice |

---

[1] *Two types of Mongol and Turkman mobile dwelling.*

	but to make peace
	or perish.
TUQAI KHÂN:	At the corpse-count that day
	your ten Generals lent you their dead
	to make your corpses more than mine.
	That was the trick you played.
	Thus you grabbed the honours of the war
	and took Ây Bânu away from me.
TUY KHÂN:	No Tuqâi.
	It was her father
	who recommended me to her.
	At his death
	you and I threw javelins.
	Out of four draughts of wine
	each time
	we gave one to the earth.
	Each time
	after six javelin throws
	we slaughtered a game.
TUQAI KHÂN:	The day my eyes fell upon her
	my heart was torn in twain.
	But it was too late
	for her father had already given you
	her hand.
	She could not see the wistful eyes
	that gazed at her
	from behind the helm.
	The eyes, thereafter
	tearful at her loss.
TUY KHÂN:	*[Struggling]*

	May your mouth be crushed! Have you come to my house as guest or robber? You treacherous usurping usurer! For what foolish absurdity would you shed my blood?
TUQAI KHÂN:	You asked me to your house as a guest you guest-killer treating your guest as a trapped bird: giving it food and water first then putting a knife to its throat!

[Qâii Bâyât, crestfallen, returns.]

QÂII BÂYÂT:	Monstrous! Just like arrows flying off the bow or water in a sieve.
DINKIZ:	Speak before you die with the worst tortures of hell! Where are these Generals hiding?
TUY KHÂN:	*[Pleased]* Hah!
QANQRÂT:	Is it not that they fled when they found you in fetters?
TUY KHÂN:	While they're at liberty there is hope for me.

[Inânj and Bâyâvot enter.]

INÂNJ:	Twisting lanes and winding alleys

| | swallowed them up
one by one.
They're like game now
lurking unseen in the woods. |
|---|---|
| BÂYÂVOT: | The drum-beats of alarm
made the people assemble.
Now they know they have a new ruler
and yet they wonder
at the fate of the old one.
What shall we do with Tuy Khân? |
| TUQAI KHÂN: | What shall we do with Tuy Khân?
Hah, Tuy Khân?
What shall we do with Tuy Khân? |
TUY KHÂN:	Whatever you take to be his fate.
TUQAI KHÂN:	So, you look fate straight into the eye!
TUY KHÂN:	Like a man!
TUQAI KHÂN:	Fate shall break you
like a dried twig
before closing your book.
Now what could be the most terrible torture?

[Commanders wondering.]

Fetch me quill and paper!
The most terrible torture? |
| DINKIZ: | Quill and paper. |
| TUQAI KHÂN: | *[Dictates]*
Ây Bânu
abiding now in Târom of Kalât |

             on seeing this missive
             which bears the seal of Tuy Khân
             shall mount her domed litter
             and descend on her Shabestân[1].

TUY KHÂN: *[Struggling]*
             She shall journey
             over my dead body!

TUQAI KHÂN: To my Shabestân!

TUY KHÂN: *[Beseeching]*
             Treat me as a man should be treated!

TUQAI KHÂN: I'll treat you as a woman should be
             treated!
             Fetch a mirror, quick!
             Call a tire-woman!
             Scissors and razors!
             Remove his beard
             and make him look like a female!
             Rub rouge to his cheeks
             women's rouge and powder!

TUY KHÂN: No!

TUQAI KHÂN: His helmet.
             His coat of mail.
             Girdle.
             Sword and shield.
             Put them all
             on a long-haired
             bare-headed dummy!
             Dress him in a gaudy woman's dress
             and decorate him like a whore!

---

[1] *Sleeping quarters.*

TUY KHÂN:	*[Terrified]* No!
TUQAI KHÂN:	What if we find him a saucy pander? Hand him over to whores and imposters —singing songs and playing the tambourine— and have him carted round the city! Let him go for cheap to any willing customer! And then... chop off his head at the city moat!
DINKIZ:	*[Steps forward, intending to calm him]* Tuqâi Khân!
TUQAI KHÂN:	Jailer! Executioner!
TUY KHÂN:	*[Falls on Tuqâi's feet]* Put me to any torture but this! Test my endurance and fathom my manliness in any hardship! But not this... not this!
TUQAI KHÂN:	Ay this... and only this!
TUY KHÂN:	Treat me in a manner worthy of Tuy Khân!
TUQAI KHÂN:	This is what you're worthy of!

	The tire-woman, the hair-plucker[1]! Where are they?
TUY KHÂN:	I'm a man bound in chains. I kiss your feet Tuqâi. Let me die the most horrible death but do not do this to me! The corpse over which I clashed with you was happier than I am now for it fell beside a flag with free hands and open eyes not so distanced from its worth.
TUQAI KHÂN:	I do not fight with you Tuy Khân. It's your legend I am after. You must be seen in a whore's attire! Are you afraid of their pinches and caresses you foul libertine? Lo and behold! Tuy Khân The head of valiant knights The desert chieftain The chief of ten Generals!
TUY KHÂN:	O Târi, my God!
TUQAI KHÂN:	They begin to sing your death everywhere. Quick! Send word in all directions! Couriers be dispatched to Khotalân

---

[1] *An approximate translation for "bandandâz", a female who plucks hairs from women's faces by means of a sophisticated manipulation of a thread.*

                    Balkh of Bâmiân!
                    to Sarakhs, Bukhârâ, Farkhâr
                    Badakhshân, Khârazm, Khojand
                    Abkhâz, Akhsikht and Takhârestân!

TUY KHÂN: Have pity!
                    Do not coax my tears Tuqâi!
                    I submit my head to your sword.
                    Bridle me!
                    Throw me down from a tower
                    but do not disgrace me thus!

TUQAI KHÂN: Go on begging
                    Tuy Khân
                    implore!
                    Did anyone ever tell you
                    that Tuqâi, The Captive-Killer
                    would heed
                    another's pleading?

TUY KHÂN: I am losing my reason!
                    Trample upon me!
                    Put me in a wall like a man
                    but do not thus disgrace me!

[He's dragged away by Jailer and Executioner.]

TUQAI KHÂN: Let drummers beat their drums
                    the town-criers cry
                    and fiddlers play!

[Exit all Commanders except Dinkiz and Qânqrât.]

TUQAI KHÂN: *[Pleased]*
                    Could it have been worse than this?

DINKIZ:	No, Tuqâi Khân!
TUQAI KHÂN:	I am pleased. Did you say anything Qânqrât?
QANQRÂT:	I wouldn't have done this.
TUQAI KHÂN:	What wouldn't you have done?
DINKIZ:	Made such a mistake.
TUQAI KHÂN:	Mistake?
QANQRÂT:	*[Cuts in]* Forgive him!
TUQAI KHÂN:	Speak!
DINKIZ:	Tuy Khân and Tuqâi Khân were two equals two men shoulder to shoulder whose names travelled far and wide.
TUQAI KHÂN:	Well now only one. One name only remains that of Tuqâi Khân!
DINKIZ:	Would that it were so! With the breaking of the myth of one that of the other also breaks.
TUQAI KHÂN:	*[Shouting]* Tuqâi does what he thinks fit!
DINKIZ:	I had to say this.
TUQÂI KHÂN:	*[Anxious]* Say it again!

	Once more! Say it again!
DINKIZ:	Two equal names! If one of them could break why not the other?
TUQÂI KHÂN:	There is sense in this!
QANQRÂT:	What are your orders, Tuqâi Khân?
TUQÂI KHÂN:	Orders? What orders? Why do you say this now when it is too late?
DINKIZ:	It is not too late, Tuqâi.
TUQÂI KHÂN:	Now that the Kalâtians know all? Why didn't you say so before? Why did you keep silent when I spoke my mind?
DINKIZ:	Your furious commands locked my jaws and the cyclone born of your pride would've blown me away had I come near it.
TUQÂI KHÂN:	I cannot tear up my own warrant. How could Tuqâi unsay what he has said? This cannot be! Woe betide him if ever he flinches! You break your silence now when I should wear a woman's dress

	if my command is canceled!
STORYTELLER:	Tuy Khân was carted about
dressed as a cheap damsel
rouged and powdered
everyone laughing at him
a dummy donning his helmet
and wearing his coat of mail.
Stones were thrown at him
and dung and spittle
while whores and children
added their instant songs
accompanied by bells and gongs.
WHORES:	Tuy Khân
your dough is fermented
your story is truly ended
there's a customer for you at the door!
CHILDREN:	From Khotalân he comes
That's a long long way
But he mustn't stay!
STORYTELLER:	Tuqâi sat down to wine
already drunk with success.
He had the fleetest galloper swiftly
saddled
to rush a messenger
over to Ây Bânu.
And he waited restlessly
hankering for news from the moat.

[Enter Jailer and Executioner.]

| JAILER: | Delivering this report
is worse than death to me |
|---|---|

| | and coming here to present it
is the same as walking straight
into the jaws of Death.
How do you expect to tell the truth
and save your skin at the same time?
Is it not more prudent
to run away at once? |

EXECUTIONER: "This is the truth Tuqâi Khân"
I'll tell him.
"At the very edge of the moat
"we were all caught in a veritable storm
"raised by the rumbling ebb and flow
"of the unruly mob.
"Now, before chopping off Tuy Khân's head
"I needed room to raise my cleaver.
"By the time I pushed
"the excited rabble
"off my neck and out of the way
"Tuy Khân was nowhere to be found."

JAILER: It was fortunate that soldiers
concentrating on the turmoil
took it for granted
that while they were busy
holding off the surging mob
the head was chopped off
and cast into the moat
where severed heads and
decapitated bodies abound.
You must thank your stars
that I was the only witness
to the incident.

It was I who cried in terror
"That mound!
"Tear it down
"and fill up the moat with dirt!"
And the excited mob
together with the soldiers
filled up the moat within an hour.
Now
if you wanted to tell the truth
you should not have climbed out of
that moat.
And if you speak now
presently
You'll be a head and a body
disjointed!
Let us report what the mob fancies!
The news of the mob-storm
and the sky-dust
is already delivered.
Now all you have to say
is that you beheaded Tuy Khân
or what was left of Tuy Khân.

EXECUTIONER: And if he asks for the head?

JAILER: The moat is filled with dirt.
Who knows what lies where?
You return to retrieve the head.
A perfect opportunity to steal away.
But if he didn't ask for it
—the storm was neither *your* doing
nor mine.
The collective exultation
and the ensuing tumult

	filled our eyes with dust
and bore away the booty.
We are bereft of our expected prize.
EXECUTIONER:	Here comes the Khân.
JAILER:	Lying
you forfeit only the prize
but telling the truth
you'll also throw away your life.

[Enter Qânqrât first, then Tuqâi and retinue.]

QANQRÂT:	I'm Qânqrât
the servant of Tuqâi Khân.
The Khân rewards you with his bounty.
The news of your good deed
has already reached him.
This compensation
for your obedience.

[He presents them with their rewards. Bowing repeatedly and walking backwards, they exit.]

STORYTELLER:	It is weeks
since the government's decree
has been on its way.
This is an ordinance
adressed to the Conqueror of Kalât
and will be delivered
by a seasoned scribe
who'll put down
the renowned name of the victor
amid the four seals

	of the mighty Tongqut Khân.
TUQÂI KHÂN:	Your fear was groundless, Dinkiz!
	You said that Tuy had followers
	and that our enemies
	weren't short of friends.
	But instead of being rescued
	the dog has already hastened
	to the lowest abyss in hell.
	And a good deed is rightly done!
	Now this episode
	should be carried
	by special emissaries
	to the farthest reaches of the realm
	—at once!
	But not to the Summer Quarters
	where Ây Bânushall be told instead
	that in preparing for victory celebrations
	her husband, Tuy Khân
	has called her to his presence.
	So
	let Qâii Bâyât set forth at once
	and bring back to me
	the good news of Ây Bânu's return.
	It's time for wine and merriment now!
	They say that Kalâtians
	have songs in abundance.
	Let us listen to one
	in praise of Ây Bânu!
STORYTELLER:	*[Sings]*
	Among the veiled ones
	only one!
	And that one is you

Ây Bânu!
You dedicated yourself to us
and so
war was defeated by peace.
Without you
today
we would've been nothing
but severed heads
piled up as minarets
or a handful of hungry souls
weeping in wilderness.

[Change of scene.]

Clothed in seven robes of black
seven veils
night-coloured
held before her
by seven women.
Ây Bânu sits in silence
behind the seven veils of mourning.

*[Invisible behind seven black screens,
Ây Bânu is brought in.]*

STORYTELLER: Behind the veils
there's only one dweller
who knows the taste
of bitter defeat
only one:
You, Ây Bânu!

ATTENDANT: I see the dust of a rider, Ây Bânu.
No more waiting.

                The awaited messenger comes.
                No, he's not a messenger
                he's Aralât
                a choice rider
                with graceful gestures.
                Here is Aralât
                the right hand of Tuy Khân
                in rank
                the commander of a thousand men.

                [Aralât enters.]

ARALÂT: Cut off your tresses!
                Scratch your cheeks!
                Cry out your hearts!
                Rip your garments!
                And cast off your ornaments!
                Moan and lament
                for disaster has struck!
                I'd rather be a mute
                than the bearer of such tidings.
                Would you sit still, Ây Bânu
                while you may know
                of the beheading of Tuy Khân?
                Come women
                console her
                as she sits in mourning!

STORYTELLER: The air is filled with lamentation;
                and cries of women reach the very
                dome of heaven.
                There are dishevelled tresses
                and heart-rending dirges.
                News follows news.

> Horseman follows horseman
> —ten in all—
> each an acclaimed Commander.

ARALÂT: Dust upon my head!
That was how it happened.
I ran away together with some others.
There was nothing we could do.
And we lost track of each other.
I have only his leg-armour with me.

ATTENDANT: Messenger after messenger, Ây Bânu!
The road is full of riders.
What shall I do?
Will they be granted audience?
Or shall I pitch
the black tent of mourning?

ÂY BANU: Let them come
one by one!

[As Ây Bânu rises, women, ululating, run out in different directions, followed by black veils, from behind which Ây Bânu appears.]

ÂY BANU: Aralât, the right-hand
are you not?
Will you help me Aralât?

ARALÂT: What shall I say Ây Bânu?
There can only be
but one remedy.
Raise your hands to heavens
call for the soul of Tuy Khân
and ask it for a way out.
Order four drums to be beaten loud.

	And between the four drums put portions of broiled meat and wine! The hungry soul of Tuy Khân wherever it may be shall descend to this table. Ask it then to show you the way.
ÂY BANU:	Is this how you'd help me, Aralât? Am I now to spread a table for ghosts?
ARALÂT:	What's on your mind, Ây Bânu?
ÂY BANU:	If Tuy Khân is broken Tuqâi could be broken too.
ARALÂT:	Kalât with its seven walls protects him.
ÂY BÂNU:	I did not say it was easy... Will you help me Aralât?
ARALÂT:	We have neither catapults nor mangonels.
ÂY BÂNU:	Would you abandon Kalât?
ARALÂT:	What is this? Revenge?
ÂY BANU:	This is my star. I shall grab it or it will destroy me!
ARALÂT:	Ây Bânu dazzles my eyes.
ÂY BANU:	And you do not hide it.
ARALÂT:	I could not

	no matter how hard I tried. For a man such as I who served Tuy Khân for the love of Ây Bânu no pain is greater than her separation.
ÂY BÂNU:	Our gain is equal to our suffering.
ARALÂT:	What shall I gain?
ÂY BÂNU:	The vacant half of my bed.
ARALÂT:	Almighty God!
ÂY BÂNU:	Victory is the condition.
ARALÂT:	Ây Bânu and I side by side? Then come what may death even! No matter. I am at your feet Ây Bânu.
ÂY BÂNU:	You are my right hand.
ARALÂT:	And if victory eludes us I shall die beside you. Now let there be a bond between us. Give something and take something in return! Thus the compact shall be sealed.
ÂY BÂNU:	What's this?
ARALÂT:	His leg-armour

	a leathern, quilted apron.
ÂY BÂNU:	In exchange this silken apron of mine.
ARALÂT:	Two tokens of a bond between us!
ÂY BÂNU:	Should this secret escape your tongue you may only dream of my bed.
ATTENDANT:	Here comes Gur Khân Beyg Tuy Khân's left arm.
ÂY BÂNU:	The Red Tent, Aralât. Have it pitched by servants and let there be a gathering for deliberation!

[To Attendant.]

	Where? Where is he?
ATTENDANT:	He's restless.

[Aralât gone, Gur Khân, agitated, enters.]

GUR KHÂN:	Still here, Ây Bânu? Why, you should fly! Let tents be struck and palanquins be brought forth! Put together a caravan and hasten to some place far away from Tuqâi —or else you shall be made captive.

ÂY BÂNU:	I know the story.
GUR KHÂN:	Believe me Ây Bânu I could not bear to watch…
ÂY BÂNU:	His armour on a dummy!
GUR KHÂN:	I seized it and brought it here.
ÂY BÂNU:	A dummy made of cane and straw with a woman's tresses!
GUR KHÂN:	I should weep tears of blood, Ây Bânu. I was among the crowd and I saw him on the cart. With a grin painted on his face he was weeping.
ÂY BÂNU:	My name be changed if I don't do worse than that!
GUR KHÂN:	Worse than that cannot be!
ÂY BÂNU:	That we shall see in Kalât.
GUR KHÂN:	Going back to Kalât will end in death!
ÂY BÂNU:	For Tuqâi.
GUR KHÂN:	This is madness!
ÂY BÂNU:	What have we gained from reason?
GUR KHÂN:	We have neither a real army nor a talent of gold.

ÂY BÂNU:	Only woes, only woes!
GUR KHÂN:	What hope is there for me?
ÂY BÂNU:	To be my bed-mate!
GUR KHÂN:	What did you exactly say?
ÂY BÂNU:	You heard me right.
GUR KHÂN:	I lose my wits! Will you keep your promise?
ÂY BÂNU:	Will you keep to my side?
GUR KHÂN:	Then this is our compact!
ÂY BÂNU:	Only if we win!
GUR KHÂN:	What if we lose?
ÂY BÂNU:	You shall die beside me!
GUR KHÂN:	A sweet death it'll be! But all in all why should we not win? Ây Bânu are you not jesting?
ÂY BÂNU:	Am I in a position to jest having lost a husband who was the ruler of Kalât? And my name so cruelly linked with his disgrace?
GUR KHÂN:	I make my covenant with you to avenge this shame!
ÂY BÂNU:	Give me a token!
GUR KHÂN:	His armour!

ÂY BÂNU:	Take this tunic and hide it! Speak of this to anyone and I'll deny the compact.
GUR KHÂN:	How could I speak of it since my comrades shall tear me to pieces if they knew?
ATTENDANT:	And now Suldus Khân The Standard-Bearing General.
ÂY BÂNU:	Outside you shall find Aralât who has men under his command. Go to the Consultation Tent and wait! We must raise an army. *[To Attendant.]* Tell Suldus to come in! *[Gur Khân gone, Suldus enters.]* Is it true that I should cover my head in black?
SULDUS:	Have you heard, Ây Bânu?
ÂY BÂNU:	Is it true —what I have heard? In a whore's habit? With rouge and powder on his cheeks?
SULDUS:	He could not be recognized.

ÂY BÂNU:	Beardless? And with a woman's head-gear?
SULDUS:	I am glad you were not there.
ÂY BÂNU:	I shall be!
SULDUS:	At the site of the massacre?
ÂY BÂNU:	You must show me every street he was made to pass and every corner he was forced to cross! In what clothes which cart and what direction.
SULDUS:	I... show you? No! Kalât is now in the grip of a muderous pack and there's no way back to it. I have only come to offer condolences. And I have with me the pieces that shielded his arms in battle. I bought them from the man who had stolen them at the moat.
ÂY BÂNU:	What price?
SULDUS:	Three Ilkhânies.
ÂY BÂNU:	I give you four for them!
SULDUS:	I am a General not a merchant!

ÂY BÂNU: Then be what you say you are!

SULDUS: Am I not?

ÂY BÂNU: Are you?
Then why speak only of condolences and...

SULDUS: Farewell!

ÂY BÂNU: Condolences... and farewell...
What enormous tasks for a General!
Farewell then, Suldus Khân!

SULDUS: I've never suffered contempt.

ÂY BÂNU: The mace must suit the warrior!

SULDUS: Ây Bânu had no fondness for Tuy Khân.
I've always wondered
if she'd ever loved anyone!

ÂY BÂNU: I'll love the one
who'd throw that head
at my feet
like a polo ball
hit by a bat!

SULDUS: Give me time.

ÂY BÂNU: Only until you pass through this door.

SULDUS: What should I do with a tongue
that disobeys my heart?

ÂY BÂNU: Tie it!
Your other tongues
Have already revealed your secret to me.

SULDUS: Have they, truly?

ÂY BÂNU:	The trembling of your hands... The pallor of your cheeks... They spoken volumes!
SULDUS:	How truthful they have been! But have they truly told you everything? But no! How can I put myself under a woman's command?
ÂY BÂNU:	You were not born of yourself, Suldus. If you ask me for the love I denied Tuy Khân walk with it! March before me beside me or behind me —towards Kalât! And I shall promise you...
SULDUS:	Speak no more!
ÂY BÂNU:	What does a lover Demand of his mate?
SULDUS:	Would that I were awake and not drunk! Indeed I shall march towards Kalât At your feet! Give me a token, Ây Bânu to fortify my heart!
ÂY BÂNU:	*[Gives and takes]* How do they wear this? A woman's wrist-band

	is worn the same way.
SULDUS:	The pact is concluded.
ÂY BÂNU:	If it is revealed before fulfillment it shall never be fulfilled.
SULDUS:	I seal my lips but I cannot stop my heart. Tell me when shall we attack?
ÂY BÂNU:	Outside In the Red Tent attack is waiting to be commanded. Its mouth is made of a trumpet Its claws of javelins and arrows. Daggers and swords make it look like a porcupine.

[Exit Suldus.]

Go Suldus!
I know what none of you knows.
The secret passage to Kalât
known only to my unhappy father once.

ATTENDANT: Here comes the Head Counsellor,
Qarâ Khân
The seasoned rider
who is
as usual
a league ahead of his companions.
Come Qarâ Khân!

QARÂ KHÂN: *[Prostrates himself on entering]*
Forgive me, Ây Bânu!

[Ây Bânu walks away from him.]

The fault was mine.

ÂY BÂNU: I need men
upright on their feet
not down on their knees!

QARÂ KHÂN: *[Rises]*
All along the way
I have been asking myself
if I were responsible
for Tuy Khân's death.

ÂY BÂNU: What is the meaning of this?

QARÂ KHÂN: I was against it all!

ÂY BÂNU: You're a wise man
proficient with your pen.
On his side
you were as brilliant
in using your sword
as you were
in running your pen on paper.
Blood flowed
from the tip of your pen
as from the edge of your sword.
Why is it that now
you're good only at stammering?

QARÂ KHÂN: It was a foul feast, Ây Bânu
And I had put down
with that same blood of my pen
a full account of it
on parchment.
The black-souled Tuy Khân

	had indeed plotted the murder of Tuqâi. To dispatch the letter I tied it to a pigeon's leg. But the pigeon was captured by an alien hawk just as it took off. And vultures began to circle around as they smelt blood. Alone, I could not fight so, I turned tail. Woe is me for turning my back to the enemy. Some of us were ashamed of the conspiracy and to us came to pass that which was shameful: a conspiracy.
ÂY BÂNU:	Ah, the death of Tuy Khân should not be recounted with groans. He deserves an epic ode. Call up every horseman you command. Order drums to be beaten and preparations to be made. Summon all to the battle that is soon to be fought with treacherous Tuqâi!
QARÂ KHÂN:	To fight with the Captive-Killer Khân? The dragon sitting astride the saddle? No, Ây Bânu! Despite your boundless courage you're no match for Tuqâi.

ÂY BÂNU: Now what's your design?
To fill my breast with terror
or to banish fear from my heart?

QARÂ KHÂN: Why choose what is profitless?
Why speak of the impossible?

ÂY BÂNU: Appalled though you are
by the shedding of Tuy Khân's blood
would you have no vengeance
no retribution
nothing?
Can you therefore prove to me
That you're no proxy to someone?

QARÂ KHÂN: I'll make you a gift of my head
if that's proof enough!
Here's my neck:
strike!
And if not
I shall take to my horse.
Farewell!

ÂY BÂNU: Go your way, Qarâ Khân!
But know that your way
one day
will lead to Kalât.

[Qarâ Khân stops.]

You'll be lost
if you run away from me!
And in trying to find your way
you'll find me again!
Am I not right?

QARÂ KHÂN:	Woe is me!
ÂY BÂNU:	Where, then, are your odes in praise of Ây Bânu?
QARÂ KHÂN:	Then you know…
ÂY BÂNU:	The songs of the unknown poet in praise of a woman Called Hayât Bânu, the Lady of Life. In the letters I received from Tuy Khân but penned by yourself I recognized the poet. Wasn't that what you wanted? Come! For shame, Qarâ Khân you cannot hide from me!
QARÂ KHÂN:	God forgive me!
ÂY BÂNU:	Are you not glad to have delivered your master to his executioner?
QARÂ KHÂN:	Don't disgrace me, Ây Bânu! Do not undo me! Do not drive me to madness! Yes, in truth I am glad… and sad at the same time!
ÂY BÂNU:	Banish sadness and let epic odes be chanted! The death of Tuy Khân mustn't be soaked in tears! Let swords be burnished and alarms, beaten!

	You'll be pleased with your temptation the day I share my pillow with you and you find that Ây Bânu is above all a woman.
QARÂ KHÂN:	Ây Bânu raises me to high heavens.
ÂY BÂNU:	Not before Tuqâi is dead!
QARÂ KHÂN:	May my pen break if it doesn't inscribe his death with his own blood!
ÂY BÂNU:	Death itself be damned if it takes no notice of your bloody inscription! Ah, is this not Tuy Khân's foot-wear?
QARÂ KHÂN:	His only souvenir.
ÂY BÂNU:	My slippers for it!
QARÂ KHÂN:	In this transaction I'm not a loser. Now there's truly a bond between us!
ÂY BÂNU:	The tongue that turns this private pact into a common tale shall be cut off.
ATTENDANT:	Audience now for the Standard-Bearing General.
ÂY BÂNU:	Oyerât? Go Qarâ Khân. Do not tarry! From the Red Tent

pronouncements
redder than the Red Tent itself
shall reach my ears
within an hour.

[Qarâ Khân is gone.]

You all seek the woman you have lost.
Ah, but what do I do?
Why this sound of trumpet?

ATTENDANT: Hark, the valiant Commander is at the door

[Enter Oyerât.]

ÂY BÂNU: Ah, Oyerât!

OYERÂT: Your enemies laugh at you.

ÂY BÂNU: So you do hear them?

OYERÂT: Tangari[1] protect you!
If he's gone
you're here.
Ay, the enemy mocks us
because we've quit the war
and run away.

ÂY BÂNU: It is good to hear their laughter!

OYERÂT: Shame on me!
They put his armor on a dummy
a dummy stuffed with straw!

ÂY BÂNU: Your hands were tied
—I know.

---

[1] *One of the two Mongol gods.*

| | And bonds
totally broken. |
|---|---|
| OYERÂT: | No, no, no!
I did not believe in what was happening!
Whispering the name of Tangari
left alone
dazed and helpless
I heard the crier shout
"Lay down your swords!"
Then came the decree
sealed with his seal.
A tumult rose in the camp.
And swords and oaths decided the issue.
He who cried out in protest
found himself in fetters
but those who swiftly delivered their swords
were set free.
Some hesitated
and had to settle for slaps and blows. |
| ÂY BÂNU: | O happy remembrance of war! |
| OYERÂT: | Do not take Oyerât for dead!
I shall return to Kalât
As one among your guard.
I'll play havoc with them
Close their chapter
Obliterate their remains
And keep their gallows standing
For birds to nestle on!
With you I repeat the oath
That I had taken with Tuy Khân. |

ÂY BÂNU: What do you expect in return?

OYERÂT: Nothing.

ÂY BÂNU: None?

OYERÂT: I am an aged man
unsightly
with sword-scars on my brow.

ÂY BÂNU: So, you want nothing from me?

OYERÂT: What if I say I do?

ÂY BÂNU: Then I'll grant your wish.

OYERÂT: You cannot be telling the truth.

ÂY BÂNU: I can
if *you* are telling the truth!

OYERÂT: Every bone in my body cries out for combat
for I am in love a hundred times
with every whisp of your hair!

ÂY BÂNU: Never gaze at me so
in public!

OYERÂT: The fault is yours, Ây Bânu
for you fill my eyes with wonder!

ÂY BÂNU: Every scar on your face
is a sign of manliness, Oyerât!
Sword-wounds
have not injured your soul.

OYERÂT: You're a true woman, Ây Bânu
even if your words were false.
No song has ever sounded sweeter to

	my soul.
ÂY BÂNU:	Breathe a whisper in my ear, Oyerât!
OYERÂT:	Manacled! In fetters!
ÂY BÂNU:	Dead or alive?
OYERÂT:	Flayed! Stuffed with straw!
ÂY BÂNU:	May restful sleep abandon you, Tuqâi!
OYERÂT:	Here's the shield of Tuy Khân, my Lady.
ÂY BÂNU:	This mirror for it!
OYERÂT:	In it there's only your face.
ÂY BÂNU:	In it only observe your secret promise which, if you reveal mine shall break like a mirror.
OYERÂT:	Even if my heart breaks this mirror shall stay intact.
ÂY BÂNU:	They await you at the Council in the Red Tent topped with colours of alarm. Go Oyerât! They blow the horn. Someone is coming. Go!
ATTENDANT:	Qâidu Khân!

ÂY BÂNU:	What did I say? So he has come!
	[Exit Oyerât.]
ATTENDANT:	Enters Qâidu Khân the heart of the army the high-born General from Câlanjar!
ÂY BÂNU:	Have you come to congratulate me, Qâidu and to scatter coins of silver and gold wishing joy to us all?
QÂIDU:	Be this far from me! For I've been at the moat and heard the dismal roar rising from the mob that had seen blood. Even through the dust raised by the storm I detected my own terror in the terrified look of my comrades. The vicious, treacherous horde treated him like a whore! I could do nothing but steal this Caftân from the man who had stolen it from another man.
ÂY BÂNU:	Why this lamentation?
QÂIDU:	I cannot bear to watch the mighty fall. It was I to whom he cried "Stay not! Go! Run!" I saw him in shackles

	and was the last to see him in a man's habit.
ÂY BÂNU:	O that your eyes were unsullied. Did it not all make you glad?
QÂIDU:	What question is this?
ÂY BÂNU:	You had been defeated by him...
QÂIDU:	In the battle over Ây Bânu!
ÂY BÂNU:	The dowry you proposed was less than half of what he offered.
QÂIDU:	I gave what I had but he gave what he had plundered.
ÂY BÂNU:	He also plundered me.
QÂIDU:	I felt no rancour.
ÂY BÂNU:	But you waited.
QÂIDU:	Without hatred.
ÂY BÂNU:	And you longed.
QÂIDU:	I waited for an opportunity.
ÂY BÂNU:	That opportunity has presented itself at last and its name is: Tuqâi! Grab it, Qâidu at once!
QÂIDU:	Do not take Tuqâi for a toy!
ÂY BÂNU:	There's only one way to get at him.

QÂIDU:	The road to Kalât!
ÂY BÂNU:	Take it and capture my bed!
QÂIDU:	You're setting fire to my soul!
ÂY BÂNU:	Burn and keep the fire secret. Otherwise forget the name of Ây Bânu!
QÂIDU:	Take the whole of Câlanjar as your dowry!
ÂY BÂNU:	I shall make a gift of it to its people. But let us vouchsafe our secret pledge with a more immediate exchange of tokens. For Tuy's Caftân I'll give you this cloak.
QÂIDU:	I cannot believe this yet.
ÂY BÂNU:	Five commanders are already in the red tent Deliberating on the battle That'll be the doom of Tuqâi, tomorrow. Join them Give them a hand And you'll recover your confidence!
QÂIDU:	I shall try my utmost.
ATTENDANT:	What shall I say to the hasty Ur Khân whose mount has not had a moment's rest since his precipitate departure from

	Kalât, today?
ÂY BÂNU:	Let his horse be cared for and himself enter.

[Qâidu is already gone as Ur Khân enters.]

UR KHÂN:	I see that ill tidings have arrived sooner than I. It seems that calamities ride fleeter mounts. What am I to call you today, Ây Bânu since you're a gazelle bereft of your mate? Some take pleasure in mourning and some thirst for blood. Avengers long for retribution and lamenters are made helpless by their grief. But I, Ur Khân, put to you a question: How can you be won over, Ây Bânu? I mean to know about the ruler that you shall choose for Kalât!
ÂY BÂNU:	You're too bold, my friend. Others plod their way on foot while you speed on as if borne along by a winged horse.
UR KHÂN:	Others are blind lovers while I am a discerning wise man. I happen to notice what the others miss. Whoever you decide to raise shall rise to heavens

| | and those you disregard
shall fall into dust.
He who is your choice
shall be the possessor of Kalât! |
|---|---|
| ÂY BÂNU: | Your fancy flashes faster than lightning.
Forgetful of Tuqâi's steely hold on Kalât
you crave the throne he leans on! |
| UR KHÂN: | Think of Tuqâi as an already defeated enemy
his golden dreams turned to cobwebs.
Violent and sudden death
shall soon befall him
through the secret plotting
of our confederates. |
| ÂY BÂNU: | No, Ur Khân.
We are not rats
lying in wait
in the dark
to sink our teeth furtively
in his flesh.
Our horses are saddled
and we shall mount them presently.
We beat the alarm
in full daylight. |
| UR KHÂN: | So you've taken to arms, Ây Bânu!
I didn't know. |
| ÂY BÂNU: | Yes Ur Khân
we shall be attacking soon.
Away from Kalât
I cannot feast and be happy
and |

| | in my fancy
lean against the throne
on which another is seated. |
|---|---|
| UR KHÂN: | No, no, no!
I cannot make a gift of my life to
Tuy Khân
for I haven't bought it cheap.
Ready with his sword
he sits within the citadel of power.
As for you, Ây Bânu
listen to the voice of experience
and do not venture into fire
for if I were to allegorize Tuqâi
I would call him
a raging dragon. |
| ÂY BÂNU: | Ah, Tuy Khân
could you have ever dreamt
that your own very limbs
might one day
sing the praise of your enemy? |
| UR KHÂN: | What praise?
Why, since Tuy Khân's demise
the valiant Tuqâi has had no peer
but the one
who stands now
before your very eyes. |
| ÂY BÂNU: | You're nothing but a braggart, Ur Khân
a swaggering loud mouth! |
| UR KHÂN: | Is it not by mischance
that he sits in fortified safety
while we roam the wilds of woe? |

	Yet your venture is alien to reason for it entails challenging the man who sits in a steel fortress with wooden daggers.
ÂY BÂNU:	Enough! Give me your sword, Ur Khân!
UR KHÂN:	I must have something in exchange for it!
ÂY BÂNU:	Name your price! Shall I give you a piece of land or a house?
UR KHÂN:	Do not chide me, Ây Bânu!
ÂY BÂNU:	A peerless gem?
UR KHÂN:	No!
ÂY BÂNU:	A slavonian slavegirl, then?
UR KHÂN:	Stop!
ÂY BÂNU:	What is it that you want, then?
UR KHÂN:	God have mercy on me. It is you that I want!
ÂY BÂNU:	God have mercy on you! Well then. Take me!
UR KHÂN:	O my poor heart!
ÂY BÂNU:	But the covenant depends on Tuy Khân's blood.
UR KHÂN:	This is the charm that'll make my horse

	gallop the fastest!
ÂY BÂNU:	Charm your dagger too for Tuqâi isn't one to die easily!
UR KHÂN:	My dagger shall not fail me! Here I've brought you Tuy Khân's four mirrors.
ÂY BÂNU:	Take this necklace instead!
UR KHÂN:	I gave and took. Heaven, be witness to this!
ÂY BÂNU:	As for blind lovers and impassioned souls —the targets of your mockery, Ur Khân was it not you who raised your cup at a Tuy Khân banquet to toast the health of the gazelle of Alân?
UR KHÂN:	I praised the nymph with a mischievous gaze and an elfish gait.
ÂY BÂNU:	Did you not also praise the pretty-eyed Persian damsels?
UR KHÂN:	May your enemies vanish from the face of the Earth, Ây Bânu! What is on your mind?
ÂY BÂNU:	I mean to disgrace you Ur Khân. I have paid a high price for you in order to sell you cheap —you boastful bully

	from whose eyes I now intend to draw tears!
UR KHÂN:	*[Falls on his knees]* Reproach me, Ây Bânu for I deserve it! Ay, Kalât is only a pretext. You alone are the goal!
ÂY BÂNU:	Rise for you've set yourself free. And bear in mind that you cancel our covenant if you reveal it to anyone!
UR KHÂN:	My tongue be severed if I do!
	[Sound of a horn.]
ATTENDANT:	Vatvât comes.
ÂY BÂNU:	Ah, well look for the Counsel Tent, Ur Khân.
	[Exit Ur Khân.]
	Why, everyone came but he!
ATTENDANT:	Vatvât, the Subjugator of Armies The Princely Son of the Prince of Yuzkand.
	[Vatvât enters.]
ÂY BÂNU:	What are you here for, Vatvât? Have you come to see me weep?
VATVÂT:	No. I shall not recount the hideous tale

of the sword and the neck
coming together.
I speak not even of the moat
that devoured him.
Yet
I had warned him
not to act on what he had decided;
and that the enemy was as capable of doing
what he meant to do.
But he had made up his mind.
And yet
he hesitated.
"Either drop the plot
"or stop hesitating, Tuy Khân!"
"Whom did you learn that from, Vatvât?
"Your father?
"And was he not toppled by haste?
"See how I fatten my prey
"and how serenely it goes to sleep.
"And once asleep
"opens its eyes in the next world?
"Look how readily it sits at the table
"and once seated
"finds its own head... on the tray!"
I told him that in a conspiracy
there's always something
that cannot be foreseen.
"Why shouldn't we beat them to it?" he
said laughingly.
But the beating had already been done
by the enemy.
We're all being scorched now

| | by the flames he kindled.
Forgive me, Ây Bânu
but he's not worthy of being avenged. |
|---|---|
| ÂY BÂNU: | Seeking Tuqâi's destruction
is not avenging Tuy Khân
but saving the Kalâtians
whose hearts my father had once united
to save them from captivity.
But Tuy Khân came
and imposed himself as their ruler
and my espouse.
Today
the bond is broken
and I
as the newly liberated mistress of Kalât
must set to work. |
| VATVÂT: | I marvel at your headlong audacity,
Ây Bânu.
I am
after all
Tuy Khân's General
and, therefore
your enemy!
How is it then
that you reveal your secret to me
as if I were his foe
and your friend! |
| ÂY BÂNU: | There was a time
when you were all my enemies
but today
whatever else you may be |

	you're the guardians of Kalât.
VATVÂT:	My father The Prince of Yuzkand despite his gouged eyes was a clear-sighted man. Yet in him I did not find the wisdom I do in you. Ah, how hideous was his death! And how much more hideous the fate that awaited Tuy Khân! I am tired Ây Bânu tired of war. What is a soldier's fate but death by the hand of another soldier? And his life... but a shattered instrument with a discordant sound? As for love I did not get what I wanted and I did not want what I was given. Now I renounce war break my sword and throw down my shield. Enough of greatness for me!
ÂY BÂNU:	What sort of a man are you Vatvât? This morning You had commanded thousand soldiers And now You're nothing but a whimpering little fugitive taking refuge with a woman.

>   Did not your father teach you
>   to abandon war
>   only when you had every neck under
>   your sword
>   and not when every sword was upon
>   your neck
>   when you stand high at the summit
>   not when dangling down the precipice
>   not in defeat
>   but in triumph
>   from courage
>   not cowardice?

VATVÂT: Could I be called a coward?
I fought bravely for Tuy Khân.
But he no longer lives.

ÂY BÂNU: Fight for me!

VATVÂT: Why?
I neither belong with Kalâtians
to fight with their enemy
nor would I rise to avenge Tuy Khân's blood
for he was not a righteous man.
What reason, then
have I to fight?

ÂY BÂNU: Are you not in love with me?

VATVÂT: I am not.

ÂY BÂNU: No?

VATVÂT: No!

ÂY BÂNU: Why don't you look at me then?

VATVÂT: I... I do, Ây Bânu.

ÂY BÂNU:	My locks, my stature and my gaze! Do I not lead astray the pilgrims of Mecca? Well do I not lead you astray Vatvât?
VATVÂT:	Indeed you do, Ây Bânu!
ÂY BÂNU:	Then, fight for me!
VATVÂT:	Would any Commander think himself undeserving of the worthiest reward of victory snatched by his Sovereign? Does not every soldier aspire to the colours of his commander?
ÂY BÂNU:	Ah, Tuy Khân rise and behold how your Commanders requite you!
VATVÂT:	Let me then proclaim in my own voice that in fighting for you, Ây Bânu I shall be equal to forty men!
ÂY BÂNU:	And here is my voice, Vatvât solemnly proclaiming that you now speak like a man!
VATVÂT:	In the women's quarters my women ask me why I don't look at them.
ÂY BÂNU:	Look at them Vatvât and do not mention my name

	until the day you make me a gift of Tuqâi's head.
VATVÂT:	That day is not far off. I shall throw it at your feet and in my heart I shall treasure your words.
ÂY BÂNU:	These two promises… once fulfilled you may enter my enclosure. Then your women-folk will know the reason you were loath to look at them.
VATVÂT:	If a token from Tuy Khân links you to your vengeance take this arm-shield!
ÂY BÂNU:	If a keepsake from Ây Bânu ties you to your promise here is her girdle!
ATTENDANT:	Nâymân Khân is at the door! Should he stay or should he go?
ÂY BÂNU:	Let him stay! And Vatvât should go to the consultation Tent where Tuy Khân's commanders are in council.

[Vatvât is gone.]

They have all come, Yâmât
except you.
Where could you be?

| ATTENDANT: | Here comes Nâymân
the dauntless warrior
who was like a brother to Tuy Khân. |
|---|---|
| | *[Nâymân enters.]* |
| ÂY BÂNU: | Tight lipped Nâymân!
What made you come all this way?
Were you moved by my burden?
Or was it fear
that moved your heart?
"Ây Bânu's evil eye
"shall bring misfortune on Tuy Khân",
you had said.
But now
misfortune is brought on you all
by your own evil eyes.
When vile Tuqânians
laid their hands on him
why didn't you
as his Pishmarg
fight for him
or kill yourself?
What is this that you carry? |
| NÂYMÂN: | His bow. |
| ÂY BÂNU: | His enemies be damned! |
| NÂYMÂN: | It is as well that he died.
Other than death
there was no remedy
for such disgrace.
Tuy Khân
a clown in a woman's dress |

an object of derision
and teased by the mob.
Before reaching the moat of death
he was more dead
than the armoured dummy at his side.
The creature I saw
had already parted with life
more than once.
He looked pale
even behind the harsh crimson of his
rouged cheeks.
The sickness of death
swirled in my heart
And my ears could no longer hear.
I was transfixed, cold.
It must have been a long while
before I turned my horse's head
and set out in your direction.
Fearing your imminent captivity
I've come to warn you
before the enemy comes.
Now it's time
to throw down my armour
disguise myself
and wander away.

ÂY BÂNU: So!
A life in exile, then
is your choice.
Well, I must avenge this blood!

NÂYMÂN: Give me leave, Ây Bânu
to lift my eyes!

ÂY BÂNU: No Nâymân!
Look at the ground
and remember the days
when you played the antagonist
doing your best to besmirch me
in the eyes of Tuy Khân.
You urged him to reject the woman
who was
according to you
"Pregnant with doom!"
Warning him about the wrath
of tribal deities
and finding evil omens in the stars.

NÂYMÂN: Indeed I clutched at every straw
to move him away from you.
But fortune was not on my side
and I found no joy in my devices.
Was there ever a man
who could bear to watch his hopes
slide into despair
without complaint
without resort to some contrivance?

ÂY BÂNU: How patient, patient...
How patient have I been!
While I concealed your secret all along
you never ceased to malign me
and to challenge me with your taunts.
Ah, you were a bully Nâymân!

NÂYMÂN: Will you give me leave
to lift my eyes, Ây Bânu?

ÂY BÂNU: Either raise your head forever

	or never look at me again!
NÂYMÂN:	At what price can I raise my head?
ÂY BÂNU:	Tuqâi's head!
NÂYMÂN:	Then, o God put it into her heart to reward me!
ÂY BÂNU:	Put it in my heart to reward you with what?
NÂYMÂN:	My heart sinks and I fear the wrath of Târi and Tangari Who, if I speak might put thunder in the sky.
ÂY BÂNU:	Do not beat about the bush, Nâymân! Tell me what you want!
NÂYMÂN:	Let me be damned, Ây Bânu. It is you I want!
ÂY BÂNU:	Tremble in your grave, Tuy Khân and let your very bones cry out! These words of his legitimize for me the shedding of his blood. Have shame, Nâymân! How could such a wish be granted?
NÂYMÂN:	*[Roars]* With blood!
ÂY BÂNU:	*[Walks left and right]* Blood!
NÂYMÂN:	Blood!

ÂY BÂNU:	*[Rotates.]* Blood!
NÂYMÂN:	*[Kneels]* At your feet, Ây Bânu I am like a Shaman at the feet of an Idol.
ÂY BÂNU:	What does a Shaman want with an Idol?
NÂYMÂN:	To grant him his wish.
ÂY BÂNU:	Does the Idol grant the Shaman his wish?
NÂYMÂN:	No.
ÂY BÂNU:	Well, I do! Rise, Nâymân! Lift your eyes and look at me and know that by doing so you shall bear my banner in war.
NÂYMÂN:	Tuy Khân be witness to this! Here's his bow.
ÂY BÂNU:	Well done! This fillet for it.
NÂYMÂN:	Ah, the arrow is launched!
ÂY BÂNU:	Guard this secret well, Nâymân! For if my given promise comes to light you should ask the Idol to grant your wish!
NÂYMÂN:	Idol be damned

| | as long as you're mine!
Tell me where the Consultation Tent is!
How should I make my vow
and shoulder my charge? |
|---|---|
| ÂY BÂNU: | Take Nâymân to the Red Tent! |

[Exit Nâymân.]

ATTENDANT:	Yâmât stands at the door.
ÂY BÂNU:	Ah, he has come at last!
Where is he?
YÂMÂT:	Hail, Ây Bânu!
ÂY BÂNU:	You are so very late Yâmât
later than all the others.
YÂMÂT:	My horse's hoof was cleft in two.
And I walked a long way
with the saddle on my back
and the bow in my hand.
ÂY BÂNU:	Thank God I have you now
dear Yâmât
my childhood companion
and lifelong protector!
You're the only one
I've trusted all these years
even though you joined Tuy Khân
at my ill-omened wedding.
I know you did that
—on my father's bidding—
to ease the agony of Kalât.
Now
at this most trying juncture in my life

it is you again
my noble Yâmât
that I need most.
Will you see to it that...
What?
You're bleeding!
Bring me some ointment, man, quick!
I shall dress your wound Yâmât.
Are you bold enough now
to dress... mine?

[She examines the wound and begins, gently, to wipe the blood around it, with a handkerchief that she produces from inside her clothing.]

Remember the unending siege, Yâmât!
The relentless snow
piling higher every day.
And bitter cold
adding pain
to raining arrows.
And tears
freezing on my father's wrinkled cheeks
when the starving Kalât
asked him to make peace
with Tuy Khân.
Remember the lone messenger of peace
who lost his way in blizzard!

YÂMÂT: O that I had never found it again!

[Enter attendant with ointments and a ewer of water. Signalled by Ây Bânu, he puts the tray down beside Yâmât and withdraws.]

ÂY BÂNU: *[Attending to the wound]*
Your snowy trek
then
saved Kalât from famine
but paved the path of my misery.
Well
what will you do for me now?

YÂMÂT: What would you have me do?

ÂY BÂNU: Some suggest I plunge in tears
wrap myself in black
wail and howl
others, siding with prudence
urge me to take to flight.
But there's a third way
which is my way.
The way of a wounded woman:
to rise in arms
Take the oppressor by surprise
and do worse to him
than he did to his rival.

[She puts the ointment on Yâmât's wound. He is in pain.]

YÂMÂT: That Seven-Headed fool
without one head left on his
shoulders now!
Here
I have his helmet for you:
A hat without a head!

ÂY BÂNU: For Tuqâi's head
I want some such hat!

YÂMÂT:	I am better now.
ÂY BÂNU:	Was it all as bad as they say it was?
YÂMÂT:	Worse, even!
ÂY BÂNU:	As wretched, as hideous?
YÂMÂT:	Compared to it death would seem like a wedding.
ÂY BÂNU:	Kalât be cleansed of you, Tuqâi! It is well that at least I have you for you want nothing in exchange from me. Women leave you cold, they say. The Lady of Alân in particular. Your heart never flutters. Your knees never shake. And her love draws no sighs from you.
YÂMÂT:	Whose imagination begot this ode?
ÂY BÂNU:	You're the begetter, Yâmât And my own eyes are witness to it! You never look at women and you stay as far from me as you can.
YÂMÂT:	God take my soul! How could I look at women when I'm given over to your love? And how can I help staying far from you while you carry Tuy Khân's name?

ÂY BÂNU: You're raving with fever!

YÂMÂT: I've loved you
since I was a child
and held your horse's stirrup for you
and ran after you
carrying the quiver
when you went out hunting.

ÂY BÂNU: How does the ointment feel Yâmât?
Has it mitigated your pain?

YÂMÂT: My pain!
Only your father was privy to it.
it was he who taught me
how to hide from you
the fluttering of my heart
and the shaking of my knees.

ÂY BÂNU: My father is not here
to tell me if you lie
or tell the truth, Yâmât.

YÂMÂT: Didn't your father
entrust me to Tuy Khân
to enable me to be
like a shadow
at your beck and call?

ÂY BÂNU: O, how wretched I have become!
What have you done to me, Kalât?
May God punish you Yâmât
for you've distressed my soul!
Would that you'd never spoken!
Never, never spoken!
This is no time for love.

	We have our obligation...
YÂMÂT:	Towards love!
ÂY BÂNU:	You belong to Kalât, Yâmât and Kalât is no longer yours!
YÂMÂT:	Think no more of it, Ây Bânu! Kalât is surrounded by seven interwoven fortifications. Even the Mongols themselves despite their savagery did not penetrate its seamless barriers before six months of siege and delay. Now with your paltry forces how could you hope to break into it?
ÂY BÂNU:	It is past the summer-tide, Yâmât. I shall go to the winter quarters.
YÂMÂT:	Relent, Ây Bânu! Life is always life wherever it may be. Let us retreat to a place where we could not be traced! We've come to this world to live not to look for death.
ÂY BÂNU:	Will they leave me to live? Let us say you're right. But will this go very far in Kalât? Will not a horde of barbarians be dispatched to take me captive? No, Yâmât.

	If you want me
	come with me!
	If I am to be your bride
	I must first have Tuqâi's head!
YÂMÂT:	In this give and take
	who can assess my gain?
	This is no time for reasoning.
	So be it, Ây Bânu!
	Wherever you go
	I shall be at your side.
	Here:
	his helmet and his dagger!
ÂY BÂNU:	In exchange:
	This ring!
	A covenant
	—till we "penetrate the seamless barrier".
YÂMÂT:	I shall wear four whetted swords
	and put them all
	at your service.
	I shall battle the cursed Tuqâi
	in single combat
	if you so desire
	and make an end of it all!
ÂY BÂNU:	Straight to the cur's lair, then!
YÂMÂT:	May your banner break Tuqâi!
ÂY BÂNU:	Go to the Council Meeting
	and see that preparations are made!
YÂMÂT:	Sound the bugles!
	Let the dome of heaven cleave!

[Exit Yâmât. Cries of horns and beats of kettle-drums rise and fall.]

ÂY BÂNU: Ah, love
what games you play with mortals!
With all our freedom
we're your slaves...
With all our obduracy!
Curse you, Tuqâi!
Why were you late
by a single day
when the siege was lifted?
And after you arrived in triumph
why did you fail to use your cunning
at the corpse-count
to stop Tuy Khân from beating you
by one or two corpses?
And when my father gave my hand to
Tuy Khân
why were you silent?
O, how helpless I was!
Wilting behind the veil
my heart beating for you
I stood in the makeshift market
and with silent tears
watched my fate
as it was auctioned away.
Curse you, Tuqâi!
Why did you withdraw
from the archers' tournament
and abandon me
to the hated Tuy Khân?
But this is all idle rumination.

He thinks of nothing now
but the unsollicited boon of Kalât
adding the realm of Khotalân
to the region of Bâmiân.
He waits for his gain
to overtake his loss
when the Firmân of Victory arrives.
But this is all passing dream, Tuqâi.
Your palmy days are numbered.
Soon, you'll wake
to find yourself a captive lion
besieged by ten uncaged tigers
for I have promised them
what you never asked from me!

[Enter four old women of Alân, white-haired and black-clad.]

Here you are at last, old sisters!
Bid me do what I should!
There's sadness in my joy
and joy in my sadness.
What am I now?
Sad or joyous?
Kalât laughs
as I lament
just as I wept
as Kalât laughed
on my wedding day.

OLD WOMAN 1: Long may you live, Ây Bânu
and never be touched by sorrow!
For ten successive years
your father

> that noblest of men
> succeeded in preserving us
> from the Mongols
> by means of foresight
> bribes and subterfuge.
> And now
> it is your turn
> to walk his way.
> Even though you're made a widow
> before reaching your prime.

ÂY BÂNU:
I do not rightly know
if I am in need of consolation
or congratulation.
My father
who, for ten years
preserved Kalât from the Mongols
couldn't do the same for her daughter.
When Kalât had no longer any blood left in her veins
facing the conqueror, he said:
"Kalât and the Kalâtians belong to you now
"why destroy them?"
The ruthless victor
would accept peace
if only backed
by an "unalterable compact".
My father replied:
"Here's Ây Bânu
"my life's most precious jewel."
Bless your soul father!
Why, you didn't even ask me how I felt!

>   You merely said that Kalât was
>   dependant on my "yea".
>   Then, brimming with poison
>   you simply hastened to the next world
>   while the feast
>   celebrating the stained union
>   was not over yet.

OLD WOMAN 2: In our songs
there's an ogre
whose fury abates
only when he's fed.

OLD WOMAN 3: You mean when he's offered a sacrifice!

OLD WOMAN 4: You entered the bridal chamber
and he spared the Kalâtians!

[Women wail.]

OLD WOMAN 1: And now that the people of Kalât
have escorted your enemy
—your husband—
to his grave
how will Kalât treat you?
As the enemy's consort
or its saviour?

OLD WOMAN 2: *[Wailing]*
O, day of deliverance
when will you come?

OLD WOMAN 3: Crumble, o heavens!

OLD WOMAN 4: Kalâtians awaited all along
the downfall of the despot
hence their making and breaking

                    of clay ogres
                    at New Year Festivities.

OLD WOMAN 1:   But in their exultation
                they failed to notice
                that they had climbed out of one pit
                only to fall into another.

ÂY BÂNU: This is the very pit
                into which
                either I fall
                or throw the new despot
                —head first.
                Come ho, messenger!
                Where am I to find a horn
                in whose lament
                The Alâns could recognize
                my father's groans?

[Attendant blows a horn and messenger enters.]

MESSENGER: At your command!

ÂY BÂNU: Call the Alâns!
                Tell my father's Pishmargs
                who chose to stay on after his death
                that time is now ripe
                for swords of burnished steel
                to be put to use.
                Now the enemies of the fortress Kalât
                tear each other to pieces.
                Their corpses are left unattended.
                It is time to have them buried.

[Women ululate.]

MESSENGER: Onto the horse...

ÂY BÂNU: Onto the wind!

MESSENGER: I'll run!

ÂY BÂNU: Fly!

[Exit messenger. Women circle round Ây Bânu and pray for her. Attendants hearing the sound of horns.]

ATTENDANT: Trumpets now cry.
The Council has called men to arms.
Renowned heroes now arrive
—Warriors and Commanders.

[Women, slowly, exit. Enter ten Commanders, clad in steel.]

ÂY BÂNU: Well now, Commanders
your decision!
Was it hard to come by?
O, restless heart!
Tell me quick
what the plan of action is!

STORYTELLER: What truly is the plan of action?
Have they all returned to say
that Kalât cannot be taken?
He who knows, knows well
how high its walls are.
In all these regions
there's not a task more hopeless
a question more tangled

	a dream more fanciful.
SULDUS:	We have weighed all: everything concerning cavalry infantry and supplies. And whatever else that might shower the enemy with death. We'll fashion devices such as catapults and flame-throwers and commission recruits such as archers and wall scalers. But Ây Bânu…
ÂY BÂNU:	Let me not hear that there's no way!
OYERÂT:	Ây Bânu!
ÂY BÂNU:	He who has made his covenant with me knows full well that Kalât is Ây Bânu's heart. Unless that is taken this will not yield.

[The ten Commanders are startled, each taking himself to be the one on her mind.]

GUR KHÂN:	Huh, Ây Bânu must not think us faltering in our resolve. No! We have staked our heads on this covenant.
ARALÂT:	We have but a small army plucky but small! We have, each of us bands of no more than five or ten

	loyal soldiers.
UR KHÂN:	I lept on my horse and a company of choicest horsemen followed suit.
SULDUS:	Lancers came with me.
QARÂ KHÂN:	I disguised myself and was copied by loyal companions.
OYERÂT:	My followers were bands of archers and mutineers.
QÂIDU:	Some came to me with swords hidden beneath their garb.
VATVÂT:	A few feared danger and some prompted by caution took to their heels.
GUR KHÂN:	I was rewarded with a band of men with proud blood stirring in their veins.
NÂYMÂN:	Like an over-brimming bowl Kalât poured out of its gates all the frightened Tuy Khânians at a glimpse.
YÂMÂT:	I came with foot-travellers.
ÂY BÂNU:	*[To Aralât]* Now, like a string, Aralât fashion these separate beads

	into a single chain
	to bind around Tuqâi's feet!
ARALÂT:	Hum! This is the plan:

[Four Shield-Carrying Commanders cover their heads with their shields and hold hands, thus representing a fort. Aralât and five Standard-Bearing Commanders act out the contents of a scroll which is read out by Aralât.]

As the dawn begins to break
six divisions
led by six of our Commanders
pitch their tents outside the six City Gates.
Beating the alarm
they raise a tumult
riding back and forth
simulating battle and retreat:
a prelude to the clash.
The doomed Tuqâi
shall disperse his men
in six directions
in a bid to defend
the six City Gates.
At noon
five of our divisions
as if to retreat
beat their drums
and take to flight
howling and ululating.
But this is no retreat, Ây Bânu.
The five regiments

	quickly join the sixth Commander
	—I, Aralât—
	all combining
	to make a single offensive
	through a single City Gate.
	And that
	while Tuqâi's army
	dazed and useless
	is dispersed in six directions.

ÂY BÂNU: That is well Aralât.
Is it also complete?

ARALÂT: The last battle shall be joined
with help from the other four
freshly-assaulting Commanders.

ÂY BÂNU: Give me your four Commanders
and take more in return from me!

ARALÂT: What have you on your mind?

ÂY BÂNU: The Alân Pishmargs
who, for years
blocked mountain paths
and held desert hordes at bay.
They are past masters
at throwing the rope
scaling walls
and handling catapults and flame-throwers

ARALÂT: How many?

ÂY BÂNU: Two to three thousand.

ARALÂT: Given and taken!
The exchange is sealed

	irreversible!
QÂIDU:	As for water…
SULDUS:	There's shortage of it.
ARALÂT:	There's water inside Kalât but not around it. So, every man shall carry a leather flask and have it filled here at the fountain.
ÂY BÂNU:	That is well thought. Now, is the plan complete?
ARALÂT:	The truth is, Ây Bânu that hope is very low.
ÂY BÂNU:	Then, I must raise it! First, inside Kalât many men still dedicated to my father will rise in our support once they know that the attacking army belongs to Ây Bânu. So, proclaim it with drums that I am in command! You're distressed Commander because we're too few and the enemy too many. But do not doubt that only a few Kalâtians belong to Tuqâi's army. There are those in Kalât who were once under Tuy Khân's

	command but are deserters now and there are those who have not surrendered their swords and are hiding in the City. There are also those who have, willy-nilly laughed with Tuqânians but shall turn their backs to them when the time comes. Let subtle agents join the caravans of peddlers that enter Kalât and secretly bring together the soldiers of Tuy Khân!
SULDUS:	This is a good measure!
ÂY BÂNU:	While you lead away the army beat your war-drums on the way and gather together the dispersed Tuy Khânians!
QARÂ KHÂN:	That should net us quite a contingent!
ÂY BÂNU:	And then by using a stratagem behind the six Gates you shall fool them into believing that Tuy Khân is alive. Now that we have his armour we'll use it as a model to make six Tuy Khâns and frighten the soul out of the distracted Tuqânians!
GUR KHÂN:	But how, Ây Bânu?

| | They will not believe this
for they have all witnessed his
beheading. |
|---|---|
| ÂY BÂNU: | So much the better
if they have seen him dead!
For they shall die of terror
when again
with their own eyes
they see Tuy Khân
in possession of six more lives.
Meanwhile
some will begin to doubt
if they have really seen him dead. |
| UR KHÂN: | What ground is there
for doubt or denial? |
| VATVÂT: | They have all seen the cart
and watched him with painted face
riding that cart. |
| YÂMÂT: | We all witnessed the end
and saw him headless in the moat. |
| ÂY BÂNU: | I put it to you
that the man you saw
was not Tuy Khân. |

[Uproar.]

Tuy Khân is alive.
You said he could not be recognized.
You were right.
Someone else had been put in his place.
And you said that he wept

>   did you not?
> But Tuy Khân never weeps.
> You said "there was no hair on his chin"
> But Tuy Khân has a two-coloured beard.
> You said "he was dressed as a woman".
> But Tuy Khân is a man.
> You said that you saw no armour on him.
> How could a dummy
> wear the Khân's Caftân?

NÂYMÂN: Well said, Ây Bânu!

[To others.]

> It would be a good ploy
> if they see Tuy Khân
> in our midst.
> And, beating the alarm
> declare him positively alive!

UR KHÂN: Let them say that he lost one life
but has returned with six more!

OYERÂT: For revenge!

ÂY BÂNU: Besides
I know something you don't.

OYERÂT: What do you know, Ây Bânu?

ÂY BÂNU: The secret passage to Kalât!

YÂMÂT: So!

ÂY BÂNU: Not even you Yâmât
ever knew of it.
My father showed it to me
before he died.

| | It's a tunnel
that leads to the Council Chamber.

[Murmur among Commanders, surprise and joy. Attendant enters.] |
|---|---|
| ATTENDANT: | Bearing many gifts
a renowned General has come
claiming to be an emissary
from the ruler of Kalât.
His name:
Qâii Bâyât. |
| ÂY BÂNU: | Turn your backs Commanders
hide your faces
quick!
He should not know who you are
or that you have recognized him.

[To Attendant.]

Call him
most courteously!

*[Commanders hide their faces.
Qâii Bâyât enters.]* |
| QÂII BÂYÂT: | Greetings to Ây Bânu
from the Conqueror of Kalât
The Seven-Headed Tuy Khân
who makes old every new conquest
with even a newer one.
Tuy Khân sends you his sword
as a token of courtesy
and invites you to join him |

	at the Feast of Victory.
ÂY BÂNU:	*[Takes the sword]* I look forward to the Feast of Victory in Kalât. What did you say the name of the ruler was?
QÂII BÂYÂT:	Emir Tuy Khân The Commander of all Commanders with rows of nimble horsemen at his command!
ÂY BÂNU:	How is he? Where is he?
QÂII BÂYÂT:	Most cheerful and in good humour!
ÂY BÂNU:	Does he still drink much and go hunting?
QÂII BÂYÂT:	W… wh… whenever so disposed, dear Bânu!
ÂY BÂNU:	Then why are you so amazed?
QÂII BÂYÂT:	It had been said that Ây Bânu was in black. Does not the armour you wear belong to Tuy Khân? You're not dressed for mourning but arrayed for war!
ÂY BÂNU:	There are colours darker than black!

[To Commanders.]

Well, we were wondering
even before this invitation
how to reach Kalât.
You are his confidant, no doubt?

QÂII BÂYÂT: Of late, Madam.

ÂY BÂNU: Look, this is Kalât.

[Draws with the tip of the sword.]

This is where our advance guard will be.

ARALÂT: They'll be the first to tackle the Gates.

ÂY BÂNU: And while the six of you Commanders
raise a storm
which they will try to abate
I, together with four remaining Generals
—you're one of them, Yâmât—
shall enter the City
through the secret tunnel
the passage that leads
straight to the Council Chamber.

[To Qâii Bâyât.]

How's that now?

QÂII BÂYÂT: Will Ây Bânu go thus to the banquet?

ÂY BÂNU: No, I will have some poison with me
which I shall take
if defeated.
Where does Tuy Khân await me?
In the other world, no doubt!

QÂII BÂYÂT:	Dear Bânu I hardly grasp your meaning.
ÂY BÂNU:	But as his trusted confident you should grasp it best!
QÂII BÂYÂT:	Bânu speaks in jest. May Tuy Khân's shadow never fade?
ÂY BÂNU:	And if it did may it not be the only one!
QÂII BÂYÂT:	*[Kneels]* Give me leave to depart, Ây Bânu and if you would honor me with a message in reply!
ÂY BÂNU:	How would you take my message to the next world?
QÂII BÂYÂT:	I shall recount this pleasantry in Kalât. So... I should have them illuminate the City! What?
ÂY BÂNU:	Indeed, without a doubt! *[To Commanders.]* What a feast will there be in Kalât! Now let us saddle our horses and ride them fast taking the desert like a storm. And this is my message: give no quarter to Tuqânians! Wherever you meet one chop off his head!

[With one stroke, Qâii Bâyât's head is cut off and rolled on the stage. Generals are dazed and frightened. Attendant and two Pishmargs remove the head and the body. The ten Generals kneel.]

ARALÂT: The plan's perfect.
Nothing more to be said.

STORYTELLER: But to those who are just and righteous
the narrator presents the story thus:
The conqueror carouses in Kalât.
The scythe of sunset harvests the
ashen crop.
In the sky
the white horseman rides away
disappearing through the horizon.
And the black rider arrives from the
other side.
Now
a vibrant night spreads a veil
on the secrets of the day.
What place is this, ho?
The field of the slain.
A mountain of bones piled high.
The ashes of the day grow darker here.
One by one
shadows raise their heads.
Someone roams the realm of the dead.
Who is this
this tongue of the silent?

[The Five-Headed Woman, all white and pale, passes through.]

FIVE-HEADED WOMAN: When will a messenger arrive
to tell us of the coming
of the Lady of Alân
to behold our suffering
in the clutches of the Mongols?
Like wolves they tear up everything.
Likes dogs they snatch away our bread.
Sucking our heart's blood
they relish it like hyenas.
A wailing messenger should go
to tell them with bleeding eyes
of the multitude of sighs
that darken our days!
When, when, o when
will the saviour
with a mighty army come
to uproot these sons of dogs.

STORYTELLER: In the Summer Quarters
the sun is down
and under the veil of night
there are whispers.
Everyone is busy with something.
All are making preparations.
The Alâns have arrived at last.
They, also
are full of fight.
Everywhere, tents are pitched
and fires lit.
Some look to God
some to Tangari
wether behind a veil
or heading for a trench.

                The Shaman chants and the Alân prays.
                But their meanings are one
                if you hark them well.
                Resolutions are renewed
                and there's much exchange regarding the war:
                who should say what
                who should go where
                what should be done
                and who should do what?
                Who would take the guise of a peddler?
                And who should join the circle of the select?
                No, there's no talk of sleep anywhere here
                No trace of slumber in any eye.
                In the region of Kalât
                the eyes of the night are wide open.
                But how would a conqueror
                in his palace
                sleep this night?

TUQÂI KHÂN: *[Suddenly wakes up howling]*
Torches, bring me torches!
Where is the lamp?
Light up the chamber!
Close the doors and search all the halls!
Who's hiding in the Shabestân?

QANQRÂT: It is I, Tuqâi, keeping watch!

TUQÂI KHÂN: You, Qânqrât?
Where are we?
Are we besieged?

QANQRÂT: We are in Kalât Tuqâi

	The City we have conquered!
TUQÂI KHÂN:	These walls are devouring me.
	This is the first time
	I sleep within four walls.
	How high they are!
	How dense and impenetrable!
	They come closer by the second.
	It was ever my wont to see the sky
	the moon
	and the stars.
	But now
	the weight of these ceilings
	—like a tombstone—
	on my chest.
QANQRÂT:	This chamber belongs to the vanquished adversary.
	It is a happy place
	larger and warmer than where we used to rest at night.
TUQÂI KHÂN:	Not larger than the desert
	And not warmer than the fire of our camps
	Why do you wear a sword?
QANQRÂT:	To guard you, Tuqâi.
TUQÂI KHÂN:	Why do you gaze at me thus?
QANQRÂT:	I, Tuqâi?
TUQÂI KHÂN:	Why so—huh?
	Let it pass!
	I dreamed a bad dream
	a very bad dream!
	I shall know its meaning

	if Qâii Bâyât sooner returns. What a pitch-black night hangs over Kalât!
QANQRÂT:	It is not yet late, Tuqâi.
TUQÂI KHÂN:	Did he ride a fresh mount?
QANQRÂT:	Along with a lead horse.
TUQÂI KHÂN:	He was swiftly to dispatch Ây Bânu's answer by a carrier pigeon. Qâii Bâyât was obedient always... obedient.
QANQRÂT:	No pigeon has crossed the sky in Kalât.
TUQÂI KHÂN:	Only dreams cross the sky in Kalât. Ten uncaged tigers coming towards me in my dream. What does that mean?
QANQRÂT:	Ten did you say?
TUQÂI KHÂN:	Like fingers of two hands together. Hum, what mystery is there in this?
QANQRÂT:	None in dreams. But in reality perhaps.
TUQÂI KHÂN:	But, Qâii Bâyât!
QANQRÂT:	According to my reckoning he should be back tomorrow.
TUQÂI KHÂN:	What do you know about tomorrow?
QANQRÂT:	They say that Ây Bânu is hospitable.

	So, until her horse is saddled for the road she'll entertain him as a guest.
TUQÂI KHÂN:	But the pigeon. What about the carrier-pigeon?
QANQRÂT:	Perhaps it is caught by a swift-winged hawk.
TUQÂI KHÂN:	Alas! But you did say that Ây Bânu would at once prepare to depart. When should she be here, then?
QANQRÂT:	Tomorrow.
TUQÂI KHÂN:	Tomorrow's not far off. Should we not set up lights in Kalât? What is the Alân custom?
QANQRÂT:	Tuy Khân if he were still living would go welcome her with gifts and ceremony. Between battlements drummers would beat their drums and the clamour of rapturous rejoicing would shake the air.
TUQÂI KHÂN:	We must do no less. Drum-rolls and bugle-calls shall usher in a season of joy. Tell the old women to prepare the Shabestân for Ây Bânu's return! But the meaning of this dream…

	Who would know about tomorrow?
QANQRÂT:	Shamans, only! Should I call Bâyâvot?
TUQÂI KHÂN:	Tell him the dream! Wake him! Wake also Inânj, Qârât Khân, Yulduz and also Dinkiz whose every word has a double meaning!
DINKIZ:	*[Already entered]* I am awake, Tuqâi —awake with a double meaning! I dreamt your dream before you did!
TUQÂI KHÂN:	There's a taunt in this remark. Indeed, you told me not to kill Tuy Khân —I know!
DINKIZ:	Did you hope to live in a City whose residents You've turned into enemies? That was the question I asked you.
TUQÂI KHÂN:	The corpse over which I tussled with Tuy Khân seems to have come to avenge itself
QANQRÂT:	Bâyâvot is here.
DINKIZ:	He, too, has had a dream.
QANQRÂT:	The only one without a dream is the one who has not slept. And as the guardian here I have not closed my eyes, tonight.

[Bâyâvot enters.]

DINKIZ: Welcome Bâyâvot.
You are disturbed.

BÂYÂVOT: And yet
what I saw
happened all in a dream.
Where is the valiant Tuqâi?

DINKIZ: He's had a dream that alarms him.

TUQÂI KHÂN: I am not alarmed
I look for a meaning.

[Yulduz enters.]

YULDUZ: The night stands still.
Hours are dark.
Horns, blowing all the time.

QANQRÂT: Where should I go?
They're all awake.
Have you come Inânj?

[Inânj enters.]

INÂNJ: I am glad you're all awake.

DINKIZ: Morning is not far off.
What do you think of this night?

INÂNJ: A most sinister night!
For hours, my eyes did not close.
And when they did
I wished they had not.

YULDUZ: And here is Qârât Khân.

Why does he look back?

[Qârât Khân enters.]

Huh, Khân, how was the night with you?

QÂRÂT KHÂN: Heavy and most black.
The rustling of the birds' wings
and the laughter of the hyenas
agitated my soul all the time.

TUQÂI KHÂN: The corpse for which
I tussled with Tuy Khân
is coming at us
banner in one hand
and mace in the other!
I knew him by his wounds.

BÂYÂVOT: Give an offering, Tuqâi!
To quell the wrath of Tangari
offer him a sacrifice!

TUQÂI KHÂN: I dreamed of ten uncaged tigers
coming at me.

BÂYÂVOT: Ten uncaged tigers
did you say?

TUQÂI KHÂN: Ten furious tigers
unchained
savage-eyed!

DINKIZ: Something turns in my head
making me shiver with fright.

TUQÂI KHÂN: You shiver, Dinkiz?

DINKIZ: Tuy Khân had ten Generals.
No more and no less!

TUQÂI KHÂN: And we found
not one of them!

INÂNJ: Kalât is full of lanes and alley-ways
and passages that lead to crossroads.
None amongst us was negligent.
They knew their way.
We did not know ours.
And it didn't take them long
to disguise themselves.

TUQÂI KHÂN: Ten uncaged tigers, heh!
This dream is not so bad, after all.
Many tigers have
in the past
been hunted down by Tuqâi.
Ay, the Great God Tangari
who made the sky a forest full of game
also made me prevail
over all earthly prey.
Never my piercing arrow left the
bow-string
without riveting ten swift-footed tigers
together
and toppling them down at once!
Ten uncaged tigers…

[Suddenly.]

The Six Gates of Kalât
Should have been bolted!

QÂRÂT KHÂN: They were
but not easily, Tuqâi Khân.
Not before the gate-keepers knew

> whom to obey.
> And not before the incoming peddlers
> could go out
> and outgoing hawkers
> come in.

TUQÂI KHÂN: So many comings and goings?

DINKIZ: This is the City of Kalât, Tuqâi
not just any place!

TUQÂI KHÂN: The roads to the Summer Quarters
should have been blocked!

YULDUZ: After Qâii Bâyât's departure, they were.
And no courier
has departed since.
And none has arrived
but muleteers and gipsy-peddlers.

TUQÂI KHÂN: Ten uncaged tigers!
Here, in Kalât?
Would that they be buried where they hide
—these ten Commanders!
And their voices never reach
Ây Bânu's ear!
Could they have sent a letter to her?

QANQRÂT: No Tuqâi.
No pigeon has landed in Kalât.
The sky is reserved
for the flight of our own arrows
and not alien pigeons.

TUQÂI KHÂN: Put my mind at rest!

QANQRÂT: Like an inverted rainfall
the arrows of our nimble archers
shall darken the air.
Blood shall drip from the clouds
and you shall see lightning
if a single bird flies over the City.

TUQÂI KHÂN: So, this is the City of Kalât
and not just any place!
But Qâii Bâyât has gone
and not returned.
Dark thoughts pass through Dinkiz' mind
and we all stand still.
No!
Do something, Bâyâvot!
I am thunderstruck.
It seems that I walk between two walls
of fire.

BÂYÂVOT: Do not walk back the way you've just
taken!
Let fifty clamoring horsemen
gallop round the palace
and lash the air with whips!
And sprinkle the sky with juice of vine!
Let us all cry out in rage
and swing our lances round our heads
from right to left.
Then
link our middle fingers
and ululate!
As with the double eclipse of the sun
and the moon
put the black dragon to flight

	by the clamour of your drums!
TUQÂI KHÂN:	No!

[All stop clamouring.]

If Qâii Bâyât is not back by dawn
I'll lead a regiment
To the outer reaches of Kalât!
So, let everyone put on their armour
and get the drummers to stand by!
We shall go
either to welcome Ây Bânu
or bring her back
a captive!

[Sound of horn.]

DINKIZ:	What is this?
YULDUZ:	A horn…! Dawn is breaking…
INÂNJ:	And with it another horn…!
QANQRÂT:	And drums and kettle-drums…!
QÂRÂT KHÂN:	Why, they split the roof of heaven!
TUQÂI KHÂN:	Look to it!

[Qânqrât goes.]

| DINKIZ: | You fear, Tuqâi
that Ây Bânu may not come
and I |

	that she may! In my dream I saw a woman tearing down the walls of Kalât with a smile!
BÂYÂVOT:	And in mine there were giant wings in the sky!

[Horns blowing.]

QÂRÂT KHÂN:	Look! The sky is wiping the black off its face and the moon-coin has ceased to circulate…
YULDUZ:	The ashen ensign is snatched away by the wind.
INÂNJ:	And the goldsmith is about to unveil his tub of gold.
TUQÂI KHÂN:	What is to be born of the rotation of day and night? The two mad coursers black and white each, ever chasing but never reaching the other.
DINKIZ:	See what this endless noise is!

[Qânqrât, out of breath, enters.]

QANQRÂT:	The sources of the sounds are not the Six Gates of Kalât but legions

	gathered before the Six Gates! They bear banners belonging to six of Tuy Khân's Commanders!
	[A messenger, out of breath enters. Bâyâvot, Qârât Khân, Yulduz and Inânj hastily exit to put on their armour.]
MESSENGER:	Kalât, my Liege, is surrounded by glinting lances. We are attacked by a shadow army bearing the flag of sunshine.
TUQÂI KHÂN:	Be blunt, little man! This army is it large or small?
MESSENGER:	In the shifting twilight some watchmen have made out shadows in the dust the pattern of an army with a flag of fire and bows and arrows.
TUQÂI KHÂN:	Go, fetch fuller details!
	[Exit messenger. Enter second messenger.]
TUQÂI KHÂN:	With what army have the treacherous Tuykhânians come?
MESSENGER 2:	Ây Bânu's.
TUQÂI KHÂN:	Ây Bânu? Before the Gates of Kalât?
MESSENGER 2:	No one has sighted her yet

	but alarms and trumpets are sounded all in her name!
QANQRÂT:	It can now be guessed what fate has befallen Qâii Bâyât!
MESSENGER 2:	With the first rays of the sun his head has been sighted.
TUQÂI KHÂN:	Qâii Bâyât's?
MESSENGER 2:	Atop a javelin.
DINKIZ:	Full revenge!
TUQÂI KHÂN:	But six he said, not ten!
DINKIZ:	Six Generals have slipped away. And we know nothing about the other four. That augurs ill. No one knows if they've joined the others or taken cover in a hideout and waiting for a signal from their peers.
TUQÂI KHÂN:	*[To Qânqrât]* Quadruple the guards! Position troops behind the Six Walls, at once! *[To messenger.]* Match their drum-beats with drum-beats and their defiance with defiance! *[To Dinkiz.]*

Where are the Commanders?
Call them all
Qârât Khân, Inânj, Yulduz, Bâyâvot!
We must convene a council now
and quickly decide
our course of action!

[To messenger.]

Bring me news from the Six Gates!

[To someone off stage.]

My sword!

*[Messenger, Qânqrât, Dinkiz are gone.
Tuqâi is alone.]*

It is well that you have come, Ây Bânu
and on your own, too!
If only I could capture you
and tell you about my own captivity!
Ohoy, where are you?

STORYTELLER: Unable to deal
with the rapid twists
in her shifting fortune
Kalât has been dazed and feverish, of late
not knowing how to cope
with clashing passions
unleashed by the late, unparalleled
adventures.
The feverish daze is at its peak today
with the sun blotted out
by the dust

raised by horses' hooves
while rumours swirl
raising hopes of deliverance
or
fears of damnation.

[Qânqrât enters in haste.]

QANQRÂT: On the Walls and behind the Gates
troops are deployed, Tuqâi.

[Bâyâvot enters, while putting on his coat of mail.]

BÂYÂVOT: Cast off all anguish, my Liege
capable hands are now in charge.

[Dinkiz enters as he puts on his sword.]

DINKIZ: Kalât is anxious, Tuqâi.
Whispered in the alleys
the question is
"What is to be done?"

[Yulduz returns, half-clad in armour, tying a knot.]

YULDUZ: May you triumph, Tuqâi!

BÂYÂVOT: How do you take all this?

YULDUZ: It tallies with my dream
where Fire
—not Water—
flowed in streams
and Dirt trod on my head

instead of me treading on Dirt!

[Inânj enters, half-clad in armour, tying his belt.]

INÂNJ: I dreamed of wailing men and women.

[Qârât Khân enters, fastening the last strings of his armour.]

QÂRÂT KHÂN: And I dreamed of a dead man
who had left his grave.

BÂYÂVOT: In the surrounding regions
no one knew
of such an army.
every living creature
seems to have crept out of its hole
to get hold of a banner
and join Ây Bânu's motley train.

TUQAI KHÂN: You are my only enemy, Ây Bânu
whose death I do not crave!
None of your Generals
would protect you better than I.
I set my men against you
yet I'm on your side!
How then
can I preserve you from harm?
Well now Commanders
what should be our strategy
in a war that yields no honour?
Should we take it out of Kalât
and position troops
in the surrounding fields?

| | Or make them mill around
within the Walls
and laugh at their weariness? |
|---|---|
| DINKIZ: | Our laugter may not endure, I fear.
The walls of Kalât
have been raised against enemies
not the Kalâtians.
where did they find the courage
to initiate this assault?
Think of that
and see to it
at once
that all the gate-keepers are changed! |
| TUQAI KHÂN: | You mean
there are Kalâtians
who would open the Gates? |
| DINKIZ: | Without a doubt
if the war lasts long! |
| YULDUZ: | And why not?
After all
Ây Bânu is returning home. |
| DINKIZ: | Our men are now more concerned
about what lurks
behind their backs
than what they find
before their eyes.
Perhaps no one has told you, Tuqâi
that since yesterday
we have found
here and there
corpses of drunken soldiers. |

TUQÂI KHÂN: Why wasn't I told?

DINKIZ: Hear it now!
Brought face to face with an enemy
you know where you stand.
You either kill
or get killed!
But it is a waste of death
if you cannot know
where and when
or by what hand
the dagger
tempered with deadly venom
is wielded.

TUQÂI KHÂN: Invisible enemies…!
Have you forgotten your title, Tuqâi?
You're called "The Captive-Killer"
not "The Enemy-Repriever".
How is it
that the Killer of Captives
reprieved the Kalâtians
and, for a small tribute
forgave them all?
I should have done
as my title demanded
counted them all as captives
put them in rows
run ropes through their shoulders
and, of their heads
made balls for bats.
All that, I should have done
and thus
made the living

| | long for death
             and forced the proud
             to rub their heads in the dust
             under my feet.
             So, they would have paid me a good price
             for the life they had come by
             for nothing! |

BÂYÂVOT: How was it that watchmen
didn't spot the enemy
last night?
Did they turn a blind eye
to their approach
or keep silent about it?

QANQRÂT: The night was pitch dark, Tuqâi.
There was no way
to make out anything.

YULDUZ: So noiseless, too!
Is that possible?

QANQRÂT: Indeed it is!
Muzzle the horses
and wrap their hooves in felt!
But then
all through the night
the windows and rooftops in Kalât
were lighted with candles
and sentries watched the feast of light
all night.

TUQÂI KHÂN: Ah, the rank smell of treason!
Now, take down this Firmân
and have the Town-Crier quickly
proclaim it

loud and clear!
We
hereby
emphatically ordain
that henceforth
no one shall be allowed
to move about in the City
without a sealed and attested warrant!
The militia are at the ready
everywhere.
Sentries are on guard
at every corner!
Safe conducts are hereby cancelled
assemblies forbidden.
Patrols are on the lookout
at every bend.
And those in league with the agressors
shall face plunder and death!

QANQRÂT: You shall be obeyed!

[Exit Qânqrât with the Firmân.]

INÂNJ: We should move the war out of Kalât,
I say
for the enemy has supporters in the City.
On the other hand
troops are not safe
outside the walls.
What shall we do with an uprising
that closes the Gates
behind our backs?
Will not then a double siege
be laid to us at once?

                And won't we be trapped
                in a two-fronted battle?
                But to take to the wall-tops, Tuqâi
                could be a different story.
                Who, after all
                can be contented in Kalât?
                There are, of course
                deserters from Tuy Khân's army
                hiding in the hive.
                The rest are those
                who smile at us
                but curse us behind our back!
                For years
                the people of Alân
                have battled hard with the Tartars.
                Can, therefore, anyone truly say
                "They are contented in defeat"?

TUQÂI KHÂN: But they clamoured for Tuy Khân's death
                did they not?

INÂNJ: They clamoured for their hopes, Tuqâi.

TUQÂI KHÂN: And they cried
                "Long live Tuqâi Khân!"

DINKIZ: Today, that is the current coin.

TUQÂI KHÂN: What do they buy with it?

DINKIZ: Our confidence!

TUQÂI KHÂN: Did they not chant
                "May Tuqâi's throne abide!"

DINKIZ: This is only noise.
                There's only a tongue behind it

	and no heart. It is just a draught in the gullet. The wealth begotten by the wind generates much income and no expense. It is a key that opens many doors and as long as it opens a door it is a key.
TUQÂI KHÂN:	But didn't the clamourous voice of Kalât reverberate through the skies as people repeatedly cried "May you prosper, valiant Tuqâi!"? That I heard with my own ears. And so did you all!
DINKIZ:	That was the voice of expediency, Tuqâi! Life is a trade and in order to live you must be a whore.

[Qânqrât enters hastily.]

QANQRÂT:	Lo and behold, Tuqâi! Ây Bânu has been sighted!
TUQÂI KHÂN:	I cannot believe it.
QANQRÂT:	They have seen her on a horse. Garbed in mirrors she dazzles the eyes of the sentries. In her own voice she commanded the Alâns to raise their flags of fire! They are preparing for a great

	enterprise, it seems.
BÂYÂVOT:	She has come, Tuqâi! Is this not what you wanted? She came but you did not let her in!
TUQÂI KHÂN:	Let us go and see!
MESSENGER 1:	Tuqâi Khân!

[They all stop. The messenger has entered in an agitated state.]

QÂRÂT KHÂN:	Why this agitation?
MESSENGER 1:	My Liege! Soldiers and watchmen… O that I were mute!
TUQÂI KHÂN:	Speak, man!
MESSENGER 1:	Bear with me my Liege. Tuy Khân has been sighted in their midst!
TUQÂI KHÂN:	What the…
MESSENGER 1:	Alive and in armour!
TUQÂI KHÂN:	Tuy Khân is dead. Everyone knows that.
MESSENGER 1:	They have seen him with their own eyes. A cup of wine in hand!
QÂRÂT KHÂN:	Away, Bâyâvot

[To messenger.]

Which Gate are you from

	you ill-omened owl?
MESSENGER 1:	The Northern Gate, in Tabarân

[To others.]

I must be believed, Commanders!

[Bâyâvot and Qârât Khân are gone. Enter second messenger.]

MESSENGER 2:	Valiant Beygs and Knights I have come from the Western Gate in Konâm. Do not shed my blood for I have not seen him myself. But the villainous Tuy Khân has been sighted just the same brandishing a purple pennant!
TUQÂI KHÂN:	Did we not kill him in disgrace?
INÂNJ:	With many a degradation.
MESSENGER 2:	Sinners be cursed! I have not seen him but those who have seem really to have seen him!

[Enter third messenger.]

MESSENGER 3:	I come from the Eastern Gate of Khâvarân. O that my tongue would burn rather than report such fearsome news! The ignoble Tuy Khân has been riding with his troops

	brandishing his naked sword!
TUQÂI KHÂN:	Hold your cursed tongue! How could a dead man return?
YULDUZ:	They're all mad! Who is this?

[Fourth messenger arrives.]

MESSENGER 4:	My stars be cursed for the lot has fallen on my name! I come from the Southern Gate The Gate of Târâb. Give me quarter, Tuqâi Khân then I shall say what I should.
YULDUZ:	Has Tuy Khân been sighted with his sword drawn?
MESSENGER 4:	I saw him with my own eyes with both my eyes most alive blood thirsty and full of rage bow and arrow in hand!
TUQÂI KHÂN:	*[Hits him]* You wretched flag-broken unruly rogue!

[Fifth messenger arrives.]

MESSENGER 5:	I come from the Corner Entrance The Gate of Khojand. Come to the rescue Tuqâi

| | for your enemy has come
from the Nether World! |
|---|---|
| BÂYÂVOT: | Tangari protect us all! |
| MESSENGER 5: | He roared behind his visor. |

[Tuqâi draws a dagger. Inânj stops him.]

| MESSENGER 5: | I am not at fault my Liege.
Others have seen him
shouting coarsely
clenching a javelin! |
|---|---|

[Sixth messenger arrives.]

| MESSENGER 6: | O mercy, mercy!
I come from the Hallowed Entrance
The gate of Robât.
Alas, Alas,
Spare my life, Tuqâi Khan,
For I'm a mere tongue! |
|---|---|
| TUQÂI KHÂN: | Speak then
And be flayed later! |
| MESSENGER 6: | Your men are struck with terror
for he stands alive
before their very eyes
wielding his mace! |
| TUQÂI KHÂN: | You cursed
damnable
despicable
malevolent whore son! |

[Yulduz and Qânqrât prevent Tuqâi from attacking the messenger.]

DINKIZ: Some pity, my Liege!
The man is but a mere instrument
at best!

YULDUZ: The Seven-Lifer Tuy Khân
who gave only one life to you, Tuqâi
has now returned
with his six other lives intact!

TUQÂI KHÂN: This is but a vile and fiendish stratagem.
You all know that Tuy Khân
was made the bride of death.

[They release him.]

DINKIZ: Tell me, all of you!
Who are the Commanders
leading their regiments?

MESSENGER 1: At our Gate
The Lion-Bodied Qâidu.

MESSENGER 2: The Hyena-hearted Gur Khân.

MESSENGER 3: The Restless Ur Khân

MESSENGER 4: The Tireless Aralât.

MESSENGER 5: The Dragon-Headed Qarâ Khân.

MESSENGER 6: The Army-Crusher Nâymân.

TUQÂI KHÂN: And beside each General
Stands a Tuy Khân.

INÂNJ: Once you've modelled
six images of an animal

	fashion a seventh and it begins to breathe! So say the Shamans, Tuqâi.
DINKIZ:	Six Tuy Khâns behind the Six Gates!
TUQÂI KHÂN:	Be you sixty, Tuy Khân instead of six you'll not have a surfeit of my sword! One death did not suffice you. Come then and encounter many more! In the name of immortal Tangari make haste Commanders! Go to the Six Gates and put fight into the soldiers! Patronize our legions! Give a hand to one another! Let epic chants be chanted and lives be taken!

[As everyone hastily goes, Qârât Khân and Bâyâvot enter.]

What news from the City?

QÂRÂT KHÂN: Terror runs in the alleys.
The ever-busy passages are empty
and the ever-brimming bazaars are closed.
Soldiers fear the treacherous mob
who
at the critical moment
might hasten to side with the invaders.

TUQÂI KHÂN: If delivered of this war
I shall make a universal gift of death
to Kalâtians.
A desolation
total
sparing only curs
to bark at their corpses.

BÂYÂVOT: *[Who has been chanting incantations]*
In all that
be as thorough as you may, my Liege
but only after victory!

TUQÂI KHÂN: There's no way out, Tuqâi!
You're a desert wolf
trapped like a rat in Kalât!
A thousand Tuy Khâns surround you
and there's only one Ây Bânu.

[Bâyâvot draws a circle around Tuqâi with a sword.]

What does this mean Bâyâvot?

QÂRÂT KHÂN: When a dead man rises
walls must be raised against him.

TUQÂI KHÂN: But Tuy Khân has died
a destined death
I swear it!
And that is why
Ây Bânu has come to avenge him.
Didn't they say
she was in mourning?

BÂYÂVOT: I saw her fully clad,

	but not in the manner of a lamenting wife!
TUQÂI KHÂN:	Did you truly see her before The Gate of Kalât?
QÂRÂT KHÂN:	She appeared only for a moment holding a Flag of Sunshine. And then quickly vanishing in the dust.
TUQÂI KHÂN:	Ah, Ây Bânu this is not what I had in mind. This is not the encounter I craved for. Why is there nothing but war between you and I? Let me triumph over you and I shall fall at your feet like a broken captive!
BÂYÂVOT:	Mark my word, Tuqâi! If you win this war you'll have vanquished a woman. And if you lose —woe is me— into a woman's habit you go!
TUQÂI KHÂN:	For shame stop this talk! We're wrestling with ghosts ghosts and living souls at once! Heaven and earth have conspired to forge an army headed by six Commanders blood-thirsty all!

	Let me count them one by one: Qâidu, Ur Khân, Gur Khân The Stout-hearted Aralât Qarâ Khân, Nâymân each deserving a kingdom under his command!
QÂRÂT KHÂN:	I hear the call of the trumpet!
BÂYÂVOT:	The noon-time call.
QÂRÂT KHÂN:	Together with bells!
BÂYÂVOT:	This is a drum beat!
QÂRÂT KHÂN:	A clarion call! Something's afoot.

[Qârât Khân and Bâyâvot exit hastily.]

TUQÂI KHÂN: I fear no war!
I have six peerless Commanders
all unequalled in war-craft
dealing fatal blows
and staging timely assaults.
But like myself
they are all warriors of the desert.
And this, here
is a cursed city
where you never come face to face
with the adversary
and do not know
whence the arrows come
and cannot tell where
death resides.
Does it hide

	behind the wall?
	Lie low
	in a back alley?
	Or lurk
	in a hitherto unknown dead end?
	O, Tuqâi
	have you conquered Kalât
	or been defeated by it?
MESSENGER 1:	*[Enters hastily]*
	Glad tidings
	from the Northern Gate, my Liege!
	The offending army is put to flight!
TUQÂI KHÂN:	Huh, welcome!
	Joy to you!
	Evil never touch you!
	[Gives him a purse of gold.]
	Fortune ever smile at you!
	[First messenger runs out as the second one arrives.]
MESSENGER 2:	Having abandoned the Western Gate, Tuqâi
	the insolent enemy is on the run!
TUQÂI KHÂN:	Auspicious messenger, welcome!
	You have eased my heart.
	[Gives him a purse.]
	Be happy
	and be more happy!

[Third messenger arrives as the second one runs out.]

MESSENGER 3: Greetings from the Eastern Gate, valiant Tuqâi!
The malicious tribe
retreated to the desert.

TUQÂI KHÂN: Such news is welcome

[Gives the purse.]

May your house prosper
your good fortune ever abide!

[Fourth messenger arrives as the third one runs out.]

MESSENGER 4: From the Southern Gate I come, Tuqâi my Lord.
The boastful, effeminate enemy
has taken to its heels!

TUQÂI KHÂN: Let it run and run!
Good news
well done!

[Gives a purse.]

Happy all!
Blessings to all!

[Fourth messenger runs out as the fifth arrives.]

MESSENGER 5: At the Corner Gate, Commander
the hollow drum has burst

	and the swaggering scare-crow
has taken to flight
and is fast fading away.
TUQÂI KHÂN:	O that your heart ever brim with joy!
Welcome, welcome!

[Gives a purse.]

May your days be bright
and your fortune abide!

[Sixth messenger arrives after the fifth has run out.]

MESSENGER 6:	At the Gate of the Hallowed Ground, Tuqâi
the offending horde
has turned its back
its hopes of plunder, dashed!
TUQÂI KHÂN:	*[Gives a purse]*
May you all thrive and flourish!
Stand firm and walk tall!

[Sixth messenger goes. Bâyâvot, wounded, enters.]

TUQÂI KHÂN:	*[To off stage]*
Beat the kettle-drum
and sound the clarion!
Let the Town-Crier roar and swagger
before the whole world!
Did you hear, Bâyâvot?
Victory!
What is this?

	A wound on your head?
BÂYÂVOT:	We are fighting on two fronts one open the other invisible. The stone that hit my head was cast by an invisible catapult.
TUQÂI KHÂN:	Your suffering be brief, Bâyâvot! Some ointment! Did you hear the drum? With this retreat their back is broken. And now all the rats will scurry back into their holes!

[Dinkiz enters.]

Did you hear the good news
unbelieving Dinkiz
from the mouth of the clarion?
Drum-rolls of victory
from four sides!
What's the matter?

DINKIZ:	*[Wounded]* We have two wars on our hands an outer war and an inner one!
TUQÂI KHÂN:	Some ointments, Dinkiz! Since the outer war is over let us now bring the inner one to an end!

DINKIZ:	This is not much of a wound. Do not put me to shame! I am a tough old wolf, Tuqâi my Liege.
BÂYÂVOT:	It is an easy wound compared with the ones I have known.
TUQÂI KHÂN:	Let us then fetch cups to celebrate this victory! Ohoy, the cups! Fetch the largest goblets!
DINKIZ:	What noise is this?
BÂYÂVOT:	Why do they shriek?
DINKIZ:	Is it from the earth or the sky?
BÂYÂVOT:	Creatures released from hell!
DINKIZ:	Like quarreling jackals they howl!
TUQÂI KHÂN:	What madness is this? The day has found its best hour and the enemy is soundly defeated. Listen to the tumult of joy and the roar of fireworks sending to high heaven the message of pride and victory!
BÂYÂVOT:	Are you happy that Ây Bânu has run away from you?
TUQÂI KHÂN:	Pay no attention to my unhappiness! Wise are the four Tuy Khân Generals who now hide each in a hole. It is well that they have tested my mettle.

Happy would they have been
had they not fought
from the beginning
with one such as I.
Let us have more cups!
Where are the jugs?
Fetch some jars from the cellar!
Let goblets go round and round!
Ho, what news?

[Fourth messenger, agitated, has come in.]

MESSENGER 4: A gigantic trick!
A stupendous trap!
The six routed regiments
have, in unison
stormed the Southern Gate!

TUQÂI KHÂN: What did you say?

MESSENGER 4: The rout was a lie.
The six regiments converged
and hurled at the Southern Gate
the cyclone that was borne of their union.

DINKIZ: The Southern Gate
cannot hold out, Tuqâi!

TUQÂI KHÂN: *[Grabs the messenger by the collar]*
You babbling weaver of balderdash!
Did you not say that the enemy
turned around
and took to flight?

MESSENGER 4: I did my Liege!

TUQÂI KHÂN: And you all heard what he said:

"Ghosts are set to flight
"and the invaders
"are but ghosts themselves!"
Did you not say that?

MESSENGER 4: Do not batter *me* my Lord
for the enemy's trickery.
We are taken by surprise.
The six retreating regiments merged
and descended upon us
all at once.
Kalât's flank is ripped open
by this thrust
and the steely point
shall presently reach
her already wounded heart!

TUQÂI KHÂN: Where are the other Commanders?
Call all!
Beat the alarm
and bring together
the scattered regiments!

[Messenger runs off.]

BÂYÂVOT: The Southern Gate shall crumble
before they can be brought together.
Now
what is your command, my Liege?

TUQÂI KHÂN: Hasn't my army
always been ready
in a twinkling of an eye
to turn around
and fall on the enemy

	like a collapsing edifice?
DINKIZ:	The army is the same
but there's no desert here.
This is a city
and you, Tuqâi
are not on a horse.
Besides
this is no straight path
but a complex of seven intertwined
enclosures.
In the winding alleys
there are hidden traps.
And invisible hands
may shower you with stones.
You can never know
where you will be toppled
by sliding mud
into a concealed pit.
TUQÂI KHÂN:	Hum, Dinkiz
what's on your mind?
Why do you sniff around like a fox?
How is it that your ears
are receptive to the faintest sound?
What are you expecting, Dinkiz?
DINKIZ:	The assault is not over yet.
In number they are not many.
But in courage
they are more than many.
The enemies
inside and out
are united

| | but we know nothing
about their plans. |
|---|---|
| BÂYÂVOT: | Let us go, late though it is!
I hear the beating of the alarm.
Let us go
and with a single voice
call every man
to come to the Southern Gate. |

[Bâyâvot then Dinkiz stop at the door.]

If we see each other no more
Târi and Tangari be our refuge.

[Bâyâvot goes out.]

| DINKIZ: | I had warned you Tuqâi
not to expose them
to the spectacle of Tuy Khân's demise.
They would have been incapable
of their present mischief
had they not seen Tuy Khân
your equal
broken. |
|---|---|

[He goes out.]

| TUQÂI KHÂN: | Victory to you Bâyâvot!
I shall not be broken, Dinkiz.
I haven't worn my armour yet.
Once arrayed in steel
his eyes veiled with blood
and bristling with swords and lances
Tuqâi shall step up into the stirrup |
|---|---|

and ride around the battlefield
putting ghosts to flight
and crushing the bones
of his Kalâtian adversaries.
Hoy, Attendant!
Robe-Master!
Where are they?
Ohoy, my armour!

[Robe-Master and Attendant pass across the stage.]

It is well that seven interwined
enclosures
enfold Kalât.
Fetch me my breast-plate
and my knee-caps.
My arm-shields and four mirrors.
But before that
my coat of mail!
Kalât
watch your last sunshine!
Tuqâi has reached for his sword.

[Qârât Khân, agitated, enters and kneels.]

QÂRÂT KHÂN: Offer sacrifices Tuqâi
and intone prayers!
That which you never expected
has now come to pass:
They have opened the Gate
to the enemy.

[Tuqâi holds his ears.]

	Listen Tuqâi!
TUQÂI KHÂN:	I did not hear you and you will not speak again! Unsay what you have just said! Opening the Gates of Kalât? We spent a long winter behind them.
QÂRÂT KHÂN:	I was a witness to it, my Liege.
TUQÂI KHÂN:	What started the fire?
QÂRÂT KHÂN:	Burning thistles tied to the feet of flying birds. A thousand flaming birds on the wing over Kalât —a thousand fire birds! In the sky there was a feast of fire! Our men shocked out of their senses were thrown into muddled ferment. It was the end of the world, Tuqâi the tumult of Judgement Day! As the awesome offensive was launched the earth began to groan and the Kalâtians inside flung the Gate open.
TUQÂI KHÂN:	I see only blood. I shall rub their snouts in dust!

[Qânqrât runs in and falls on his knees.]

QANQRÂT:	Stiffen your courage, Tuqâi

	and lend ear! They are behind the first enclosure —TuyKhânians and Kalâtians together.
TUQÂI KHÂN:	The old enemies.
QANQRÂT:	Under the banner of Ây Bânu they are today's friends!
TUQÂI KHÂN:	I shall drink their blood!
QANQRÂT:	Tuy Khân has been sighted beside the Gate.
TUQÂI KHÂN:	That dog!
QANQRÂT:	With six faces.
TUQÂI KHÂN:	I shall sink my teeth in his gullet!
	[Yulduz, horrified, enters and falls on his knees.]
YULDUZ:	The earth does crumble now, Tuqâi for the first of the seven enclosures has fallen!
TUQÂI KHÂN:	But my warriors... Do they not fight?
YULDUZ:	They have seen Tuy Khân before the first enclosure.
TUQÂI KHÂN:	Drawing nearer... this rotten freak!
YULDUZ:	Some soldiers have run away.
TUQÂI KHÂN:	There can be no escape in Kalât!
YULDUZ:	There is no room

	to run fast on the walls. They're coming but not all at once.
TUQÂI KHÂN:	O foul carrion!

[Inânj, terrified, enters and falls on his knees.]

INÂNJ:	To be believed it must be seen, Tuqâi. The second wall has crumbled.
TUQÂI KHÂN:	Anything else —worse than this?
INÂNJ:	Tuy Khân before the second wall with six faces!
TUQÂI KHÂN:	Hoy!

*[Roaring, he begins to whirl around,
raising and rotating in the air the two
Commanders who hold his arms.]*

Position every man behind the third wall
and be resolved to kill the six Tuy Khâns!
I shall put these ghosts to flight.
Black banner in hand
I shall sit in the saddle
raising dust from their bones
with a pounding mace.
I shall fill the eyes of the world
with dirt.
Once again
when the scattered army unites
not even Heaven can hold it back!

[The four Commanders, with drawn swords, have run out. Attendant and Robe-Master, robes in hand, have entered.]

I wear my armour.
Quick!
Temper my sword with poison!
Set flames to my arrows
and steep my lance's point
in viper venom!
Once I put on my armour
the soldiers will be dazzled.
I am indeed safe from men...
But not from myself.
What, frightened?
Why are you so pale, then?

ROBE-MASTER: I sweep the ground before your feet, Tuqâi Khân
but tell me if our Kalâtian enemies
outnumber our warriors.

TUQÂI KHÂN: What does this mean?

ROBE-MASTER: The invaders have the backing of the Kalâtians
who now throw baked bricks at our men.

TUQÂI KHÂN: They'll soon welter in their own blood!

ATTENDANT: There's clamour about Tuy Khân
not being dead.
His six lives
they say
have returned
to avenge his first.

TUQÂI KHÂN: A dog has seven lives.
You dog!

ATTENDANT: A dog indeed!
Was he not called that
when he was carted around
clad in a woman's clothes?

ROBE-MASTER: This is what they chanted, I think:
the fawn dog
when he dies
the jackal goes into mourning!

ATTENDANT: No, this is how it went:
the fawn dog
is every bit
like a jackal:
the paws
the snout
the tincture and all!

ROBE-MASTER: What I say is more correct.

ATTENDANT: I was there
and you were not.

ROBE-MASTER: It was just as I said.
And then
a whole crowd
together barked
like a dog.

ATTENDANT: Howled
like jackals.

ROBE-MASTER: And now
after all this

                celebrating Tuy Khân's return
                they howl again.

TUQÂI KHÂN: Hoy, this is all coarse ranting
nothing but trickery or fancy.
Turn your heart into stone Tuqâi
for you must now wrestle with the dead.
So, he has returned...
I am fighting with a man
whom Kalâtians
with songs and ululations
have retrieved from hell.
The Jailer and the Executioner...
Where are they?
Let them come, let them come!
Give me my sword!

[Attendant and Robe-Master, frightened, run out.]

Whatever she may contemplate
Ây Bânu is no more than a woman.
How can she gather an army?
How could the Generals of the Seven-Headed Tuy Khân
obey her command?
Unless this is a falsehood
and Tuy Khân is still truly their head.
But this same murderous monster
was held at bay
Behind the walls of Kalât
for more than a year
while today's Commander
whoever he may be

is winning the war in one day.

[Enter Jailer and Executioner.]

Greetings to you Jailer
and you Executioner!
I have rewarded you for saying
that you had cut off Tuy Khân's head.
Well, had you?

EXECUTIONER: With each others' help.

TUQÂI KHÂN: *[To Jailer]*
Then you have witnessed his death
with your own eyes.

JAILER: By the light of your own eyes!

TUQÂI KHÂN: *[To Executioner]*
What did death do to him?

EXECUTIONER: Kill him!

TUQÂI KHÂN: With your hands?

EXECUTIONER: By your command!

TUQÂI KHÂN: *[To Jailer]*
And you were witness to this?

JAILER: Your obedient servant.

TUQÂI KHÂN: Swear by this sword!

EXECUTIONER: By Târi and Tangari
from whom there is escape
but not from this sword!

JAILER: *[Weeping]*
I only tied his chain.

TUQÂI KHÂN:	And you were a witness!
EXECUTIONER:	I cannot remember any prayer.
JAILER:	Would that at least you had not spent the reward!
TUQÂI KHÂN:	How did you hack his neck? With how many strokes?
EXECUTIONER:	One only.
TUQÂI KHÂN:	Did he groan?
JAILER:	No…
EXECUTIONER:	Yes.
TUQÂI KHÂN:	So, he did and he did not! Did he hold out his neck or did you do it for him?
EXECUTIONER:	He was resigned and yet he was not.
JAILER:	We gave him a hand.
TUQÂI KHÂN:	And the head… Did it fall in the moat or outside of it?
JAILER:	It fell upside down.
TUQÂI KHÂN:	*[To Executioner]* Should you not have fetched it?
EXECUTIONER:	I did but you did not want it, my Liege.
TUQÂI KHÂN:	So you did but I did not want it. Then what?

EXECUTIONER:	Tuy Khân was dead.
TUQÂI KHÂN:	The head!
EXECUTIONER:	I took it back and flung it into the moat.
TUQÂI KHÂN:	Did anyone see you?
JAILER:	No.
TUQÂI KHÂN:	Or the head?
JAILER:	Woe is me!
TUQÂI KHÂN:	And if he was not put to death then woe is me!
EXECUTIONER:	Even so, Khân!
TUQÂI KHÂN:	And you did bury it beneath the earth!
EXECUTIONER:	Very carefully, my Lord.
TUQÂI KHÂN:	*[To Jailer]* And you were a witness to all this!
JAILER:	All the while.
TUQÂI KHÂN:	Then you know where it is?
EXECUTIONER:	How?
TUQÂI KHÂN:	Don't you?
JAILER:	There is much earth in a large moat!
TUQÂI KHÂN:	*[To Executioner]* But you did conceal it in a precise place!
EXECUTIONER:	Ah, what shall I say?

TUQÂI KHÂN: Make up a lie and tell it.

EXECUTIONER: *[Weeping]*
I cannot remember one.

TUQÂI KHÂN: Say
perhaps someone stole it at midnight!

EXECUTIONER: But what about the sentries and watchmen?

JAILER: So it's not stolen!

TUQÂI KHÂN: One of you stays
the other goes to fetch the head.
And if, within an hour
he doesn't come back
the hostage shall lose his head.
Well, which of you goes
and which one stays?

EXECUTIONER: I.

JAILER: I.

EXECUTIONER: Give me leave, Khân!

JAILER: O that I be your sacrifice, Tuqâi
command me to go!

TUQÂI KHÂN: What is the difference
between the one that goes
and he who stays?

EXECUTIONER & JAILER: None.

TUQÂI KHÂN: There is, indeed
a difference:
The one that goes
knows well

                that there's no head.
                He sells the other one to death
                to buy himself a life.
                the one that goes
                knows how to run away.
                Well then
                I ask you once again
                and I'll give you quarter.
                You'll live
                only if you tell the truth.
                If you have beheaded him
                bring me his head;
                if not
                speak the truth at once
                and release me from this deadly terror.
                Have you truly killed him?

EXECUTIONER: God forgive me!

JAILER: O, my poor heart!

TUQÂI KHÂN: Speak!

EXECUTIONER: He fled, Tuqâi!

TUQÂI KHÂN: Did he?

JAILER: Indeed.
But we did not even see his flight!

TUQÂI KHÂN: Ah!

EXECUTIONER: Here's my head Khân.
Cut it off
and releave me from fear for my life!

TUQÂI KHÂN: Why, what is the use now?
Tuy Khân is alive…

And to kill you
or let you go
will make no difference.
Get up and go away!
Remove yourselves from my sight!
Go away!

[Jailer and Executioner, unbelieving and frightened, exit.]

Hum! She was a woman with five heads.

[To outside.]

Bring me my armour!
It seems that
single-handed
I must come face to face
with all the seven lives of Tuy Khân!
But you do not know, Tuy Khân
that I possess no less than seventy lives.
And now
Tangari who are in Heaven
accept this offering from me:
three drops of vine-blood
I sprinkle on the ground
in four directions.
And these remaining drops
I deliver up to you.
Drink them
and raise invisible walls
on my four sides
to deter my adversary
from wounding me.

                    But let him be inflicted
                    with mighty wounds!

                    [Robe-Master and Attendant enter.]

ROBE-MASTER: Make haste!
                    Breast-plate.
                    Knee-caps.
                    Arm-shields.
                    The four mirrors.
                    Leg pieces
                    and elbow-pieces.

TUQÂI KHÂN: Through which door will Tuy Khân come
                    If he will?
                    This or that?
                    I shall unleash a bloody massacre
                    that will leave no head
                    on the shoulders of Tuy Khân's men.
                    I will not put my head in their halter!
                    When the day is done
                    counters shall count corpses
                    belonging to each side.

ROBE-MASTER: Hold this!

ATTENDANT: Pull!

ROBE-MASTER: Tie it well!

TUQÂI KHÂN: Ah, may there never come the hour
                    when he could laugh at me
                    in chains
                    he prevailing
                    And I surrendering in disgrace.
                    I'd be equal to any torture, Ây Bânu

                anything...
                But to be disgraced before your eyes...
                If defeat is to come
                may death precede it!

ATTENDANT: Which, the girdle or the shoulder-piece?

ROBE-MASTER: Sword-belt
and elbow-piece.

TUQÂI KHÂN: How could Tuy Khân forget
the disgrace I brought on him?
He must be conjuring up
fresh tortures now.
What would be the worst chastisement
his mind can device, I wonder?

[Attendant and Robe-Master, once again, go out to fetch some other pieces of armour but, this time, instead of them, Yâmât and Vatvât enter with several pieces and proceed, at the same speed, to put them on Tuqâi.]

TUQÂI KHÂN: Do your worst, Tuy Khân
Worse than anything that might come
to your mind!
In me the world shall find
a new model of endurance...
And I will put to shame
The conjurer of new tortures.
Tighter, tighter!
I know much about manacles
that mangle hands and feet.
And bludgeons
that crack the skull

	and rammers too.
	I even know a thing or two
	about dismemberment of a man's frame
	or that spine-chilling horror
	called Chinese Crucifixion.
	Hold out Tuqâi
	and never let him hear you plead!

YÂMÂT: Is it fastened well?

VATVÂT: Turn the hook!

YÂMÂT: Tie the cord!

TUQÂI KHÂN: I should order
the portals of the Council Chamber
bolted behind the six Commanders
to block their retreat
and leave them no choice
but to fight.
Ohoy, see that this is done!
Are the portals closed?
Ah, I feel better now.

YÂMÂT: Kneel down Tuqâi!

TUQÂI KHÂN: What did you say?

YÂMÂT: Think nothing of it
kneel down!

TUQÂI KHÂN: What are you, little man?

[He makes as if he's drawing the sword, which he does not wear. He becomes helpless as he finds out that his two arm-shields are chained together and so are his two leg-pieces. Incredulous, he struggles in vain.]

TUQÂI KHÂN:	To be taken captive without a fight?
VATVÂT:	Stop howling!
TUQÂI KHÂN:	With my hands untied
I am a match to ten of you!

[Oyerât and Suldus enter. Tuqâi stops struggling.]

Who are these?

[Suldus halters him. Vatvât and Yâmât press two lances on his shoulders to force him to kneel down. Ây Bânu, clad in Tuy Khân's armour, enters, her face half-veiled.]

OYERÂT:	Kneel down
before the Conqueror of Kalât!
TUQÂI KHÂN:	O, Târi and Tangari
give me quarter!
You must be Tuy Khân's Generals!

[Horrified.]

They are ten now!
How have you come?
From what secret hiding
and through which way
other than the fortified enclosure of
my warriors?

[He notices Ây Bânu.]

Who is this?

ÂY BÂNU:	How does the world go, Tuqâi?

TUQÂI KHÂN:	Tuy Khân in armour arrayed as a woman too as I dressed him! O, horror! You've come from hell, Tuy Khân!
ÂY BÂNU:	Indeed the place you shall presently go to!
TUQÂI KHÂN:	Huh?
ÂY BÂNU:	It's not for me to describe it. I only know that the fires raised by your misdeeds pale before it!
TUQÂI KHÂN:	Do not threaten me with your torments and this voice of yours. Why speak with a woman's voice? Is this because I had you dressed In a woman's garb? You hide your face, hey waiting for your beard to grow?
ÂY BÂNU:	You don't know, Tuqâi that death is closer to us than the lashes of our eyes. And hell is just behind your heels. Make a slip and you're in it. Ah, Tuqâi you cannot know that the two worlds together

| | are no bigger
than a clenched fist.
And every man's hell
is as big as himself.
What happened to your rantings, Tuqâi?
Your boasts
your swagger?

TUQÂI KHÂN: *[Struggles]*
My warriors have slain six other
Tuy Khâns.
How did you manage
to save your neck… Tuy Khân?
And if you did
why should not I?

ÂY BÂNU: You took yourself to be a Khân.
But in truth
you were nothing
but an agent of death
feeding it with every paltry morsel
you could lay your hands on.

OYERÂT: Tuqâi The Captive-Killer
now a captive yourself!
Were you not ashamed
of beating such a hasty drum?
O, such a commander too!
Let the world go round
and let his warriors know
that we caught him
even as he was about to steal away!

TUQÂI KHÂN: May your jaws be crushed
accusing me thus!

	Steal away? Tuqâi?
VATVÂT:	You were preparing to run away!
TUQÂI KHÂN:	I was preparing to fight!
ÂY BÂNU:	Why do you not fight, then you braggart instead of turning your back on the enemy?
TUQÂI KHÂN:	*[Struggling]* I?
ÂY BÂNU:	Be silent, fugitive Tuqâi! Put the seal of Tuqâi under this Firmân then take it out and read it to Tuqânians: "To be saved from impending death "Put your swords down at once". Bring me news of the battle. And open the door when the Alâns come to the Council House.
YÂMÂT:	The tale of this captivity must be told. I know a fiddler who also sings well. Let us go!
TUQÂI KHÂN:	Has no one among you the kindness to kill me?

[Vatvât and Yâmât are gone.]

OYERÂT:	You once called yourself The Lion of Khotalân and Bâmiân.

SULDUS:	You wallowed in your pride and your ambition knew no bounds.
OYERÂT:	Should we not offer him now as a sacrifice?
SULDUS:	What are we really to do with him?
ÂY BÂNU:	Indeed. How should we treat you, Tuy Khân?
TUQÂI KHÂN:	Worse than what comes to your mind.
ÂY BÂNU:	Did worse than what come to *your* mind?
TUQÂI KHÂN:	I had expected this.
ÂY BÂNU:	Your expectations shall be surpassed. Death is less than your just deserts and yet you shall die! Would it not make you sad to be counted as a corpse such as those you have counted at victories? Do you recall the havoc you wrought with Kalât and the bloodbath that issued from your quarrelling over a single corpse? What are you but a corpse now, Tuqâi?
OYERÂT:	Don't struggle, beast! Your chains are stoutly made.
TUQÂI KHÂN:	As warriors we are both great, Tuy Khân. So treat me as such.
ÂY BÂNU:	In dealing with "Great Warriors"

We'll follow your lead.
So, let us quickly shave
all manly adornment
off Tuqâi's face
and give him
instead
the thickly painted aspect of a whore!
We'll have you dragged around
and presented to customers.
And you'll keep cackling like a fool
in a woman's dress.
And if you jig and wiggle
you'll have more clients.
But if you sulk and glower
you'll find fewer takers.

OYERÂT: Let a big grin be painted on his face!
Put a band around his head
and make him ride an ass
back to fore!

SULDUS: A mule shall wear his armour
and put on his casque
and be ridden
by a drum-beating shrew!

TUQÂI KHÂN: I fall at your feet, Tuy Khân.
Do not do this to me!

ÂY BÂNU: Did you not do this to your host
when you came to Kalât as a guest?
And didn't your misdeed
cause the shedding
of a thousand people's blood?

TUQÂI KHÂN: I have done wrong, I know

	but save my honor now! I kiss your feet and with tearful lashes sweep the ground you tread on!
ÂY BÂNU:	Beg Tuqâi, beg! Louder! Your tears may soften my heart.
TUQÂI KHÂN:	You're so full of cheer!
ÂY BÂNU:	Indeed, I am!
TUQÂI KHÂN:	Belittle me no more! Speak to me with your own voice! To be captured by a woman! Think of my shame in the next world!
ÂY BÂNU:	Shame on me if I do you wrong, Tuqâi. Yet, I will not be your equal unless I do so. Hah, which torture would suit him best?
OYERÂT:	Chinese Crucifixion!
TUQÂI KHÂN:	Your anger is not rooted in the wrongs I did you, Tuy Khân but in the love I bear Ây Bânu to which I made you privy. You chafe at the songs I distilled from her glance and the toasts I drank to the freshness of her cheeks! By trickery you snatched her away from me. That was the cause of all that I did to you, then.

And this is the cause of all
that you do to me now.

[He struggles between the arms of the two Commanders.]

ÂY BÂNU:	What talk is this? Why now when I have ceased to expect it and not then When I did long for it? Ah, be damned Tuqâi! You have picked off my petals with your words. god bring you to your end for by abandoning me to my hangman You brought me to mine!
SULDUS:	Let them pack-saddle and bridle him!
OYERÂT:	That's not enough!
SULDUS:	Make him run blindfolded on spikes!
OYERÂT:	Something worse than that!
TUQÂI KHÂN:	I know what all this shall lead to… What if she comes to regard me as no more than a mouse under her feet? Tuy Khân, I beseech you cling to you! Do not break my heart before the eyes of one who already has it under her feet. Other than that

                    do to me whatever you would!
                    Let the whole world
                    hold me in contempt
                    but only spare me
                    from disgrace
                    before her eyes!

ÂY BÂNU: O, my poor heart
                    caught in a mass of tangled knots
                    and lacerated by his groans!
                    How long will you hold out
                    and continue to trample over your longings?
                    What am I doing in this armour?
                    What is the meaning of this scaly crust?
                    Away, cold and knotted steel!
                    And yet
                    you are not all!
                    Kalât stands on the other side.
                    I can live without love
                    but not without dignity.
                    You must harden your heart, Ây Bânu
                    or else
                    you shall waste away!
                    I shall surely kill you, Tuqâi
                    and make your coffin
                    my bridal chamber!

STORYTELLER: Ah love
                    the games you play with mortals!
                    You replenish legends with their blood.
                    Of "union"
                    you give too late, if ever.
                    As for "separation"

                you make it fit their measure.
                To him who has died of grief
                you grant new life.
                And you make yourself manifest
                on the face of death.
                You spread suffering on joy
                and bring patience to heel.
                You dispense happiness by the drop
                and measure pain by the sea.
                And when abiding in a man's heart
                you drive him out of his abode.
                Ah love
                the games you play with mortals!

ÂY BÂNU: After the drum roll of victory
take him to the front portico
and let Kalât behold
with her own eyes
that she has received justice!

TUQÂI KHÂN: *[Struggling]*
You're a black cloud
covering the face of the sun, Tuy Khân!
It was said in the songs sung in Kalât
That Ây Bânu was Tuy Khân's enemy.
This is the taunt that sets you aflame
you creature of hell!
O had I only pulled the sky down to earth
and snatched her away from you...

ÂY BÂNU: You sail your ship on dryland, Tuqâi!
Even I have come to grief
—Tuy Khân though I am—
for I forced myself on her

with a vengeance.
Had you claimed her by the sword
you would have gained nothing
but her repugnance.

SULDUS: Drag the traitor on stony ground
roped to a running camel!

OYERÂT: And let his deserved end
be trumpeted
through the whole of Tâtârestân:
from Qâzân
to the region of Qarjestân!
Let Chagal beauties
Tarâz maidens
and Farkhâri charmers
all dancing and clapping
with many a smile
and much dalliance

SULDUS: Now look at the scoundrel
shedding false tears!

ÂY BÂNU: O, how defenseless heroes are
when they come close to us!
Their reputation binds them
to a certain demeanor
but their tears
reveal them.
If I were Ây Bânu
I could have had pity on you
for her heart is exceedingly tender.
But since I happen to be Tuy Khân
I'm full of fury now.
What I will presently do to you

	shall become a legend one day. Now... what would be the worst torture?
TUQÂI KHÂN:	Come death, quick!
ÂY BÂNU:	Worse than death!
OYERÂT:	Flay him!
ÂY BÂNU:	No!
OYERÂT:	Bridle him!
SULDUS:	Have him shod like a mule!
ÂY BÂNU:	No!
OYERÂT:	Do to him exactly what he did to Tuy Khân!
TUQÂI KHÂN:	Not in her presence!
ÂY BÂNU:	No!
OYERÂT:	Pour molten lead down his throat!

[Ây Bânu thoughtfully shakes her head.]

SULDUS:	I've found the solution to this puzzle at last. Let a bludgeon be rammed into him!
TUQÂI KHÂN:	No, no, not this! Anything, anything but this!
ÂY BÂNU:	Indeed I shall do worse than this, Tuqâi... I'll forgive you!
OYERÂT:	What? Forgive?

SULDUS: Think, my Sovereign
before you do anything
as rash as that!

ÂY BÂNU: I... will... forgive... him!

TUQÂI KHÂN: This indeed is the worst
that could have befallen to me.
That my enemy should forgive me
and that he
who was about to be my torturer and slayer
should give me life
and be my second God!
No!
Anything but that!
How could Tartars believe
that Tuqâi has not begged for his life?

ÂY BÂNU: Unchain him!

SULDUS: How can you set such a reckless monster free?

OYERÂT: On my knees, my heedless sovereign
I beseech you...

ÂY BÂNU: Do what you're told
and say no more!

TUQÂI KHÂN: *[As they begin to unchain him]*
Kill me, I say
or I'll die of shame
if I am just forgiven
I shall die of shame!
For it will surely be said
that I saved my life

                    by tears and entreaties.
                    So kill me quick
                    you crafty scheming freak
                    or I'll make you regret
                    the day you forgave me!

                    [Freed at last, he jumps at Oyerât and snatches his dagger.]

OYERÂT: *[Reacting to Tuqâi's attack.]*
                    Hold your ungrateful hand!

SULDUS: *[Draws sword]*
                    Brazen, shameless, fiend
                    take this!

ÂY BÂNU: Step aside!

                    [The two Commanders freeze.]

TUQÂI KHÂN: Now I have a dagger, Tuy Khân!

ÂY BÂNU: That is well, Tuqâi!

TUQÂI KHÂN: And you're without a sword!

ÂY BÂNU: You can use it now Tuqâi!

                    [Uncovers her face.]

TUQÂI KHÂN: Almighty Heaven!
                    It's Ây Bânu
                    It's Ây Bânu!

                    [He stabs his chest with the dagger and falls; gets up; takes a step; stops; stretches his hand towards her; tries to walk up to her. Oyerât strikes him with his sword. He

falls again; gets up. Now he's struck by Suldus. He falls at Ây Bânu's feet. She turns her back. Oyerât sits on his head.]

OYERÂT: Long may you live Ây Bânu!
Your enemy is dispatched to hell now!

ÂY BÂNU: True Oyerât
Kalât is now ours.

[Yâmât enters panting, followed by Alân Pishmargs.]

YÂMÂT: Alâns fought well Ây Bânu.
Six Enclosures have already fallen.
The battle now rages around the Seventh Wall.
Fie, fie, what am I to say?
Six of Tuqâi's Generals
along with six of Tuy Khân's under your command
were all slain
in the fiercest face-to-face battle of the day.
The fallen Tuqâniâns:
Dinkiz, Yulduz
Qârât Khân, Qânqrât
Inânj and Bâyâvot.
And the Tuy Khâniâns:
Aralât, Gur Khân
Qarâ Khân, Qâidu
Ur Khân and Nâymân.

OLD PISHMARG: They were all brave Commanders.
They could have brought prosperity

	to so many lands!
OYERÂT:	They're the victims of a groundless war triggered by the rivalries of two stubborn contenders.
ÂY BÂNU:	Tell the world their names and let us mourn them all! Sound the clarion and let banners fly at half mast! Cut their horses' manes and saddle them backwards! With full respect take the body of Tuqâi the conqueror of Kalât to the palace gate and let his soldiers file past him and surrender their swords!

[The Alâns take up the body. Attendant enters, panting.]

ATTENDANT:	Joy and sorrow are mingled together. Victory is still outside. Yet a group of men and women have come to offer their greetings.

[Vatvât enters, panting.]

VATVÂT:	Tuqâniâns have finally dropped their shields. But a few dozen with bows and arrows and foaming at the mouth hound the populace.

| | Fear of death
               has turned them
               into death-mongers. |

ÂY BÂNU: Death comes cheap in the battle.
The thirsty
drink freely from this foun, Oyerât Khân!

OYERÂT: *[Draws]*
The mad should either be chained
or banished!
Friends
companions and warriors
Alâns and noble cavaliers
come!

[Exit with some Alâns.]

ÂY BÂNU: Brave Vatvât
entrust the City
to the indomitable Alâns!
Put them in charge
and place yourself in command of
the sentries
guarding the Chancellory!

[Exit Vatvât, along with few Alâns.]

Suldus Khân
search for the two murderers
and have them arrested.

SULDUS: Ay, it is time for Tuy Khân's slayers
to be given their just deserts.
The Jailer and the Executioner

	where are they?
ÂY BÂNU:	Bring them here and have them recount their sorry deed in detail!

[Exit Suldus, drawing his sword.]

	Now, Yâmât you're the only one I can confide in!
YÂMÂT:	These words are just. And coming from your lips most sweet.
ÂY BÂNU:	No time yet, good Yâmât for dalliance or repose. For while the bravest generals are tearing each other into pieces. The cycle of calamity is not yet complete. Kalât has not stopped bleeding yet.
YÂMÂT:	Other than Kalât is there anything you might think about?
ÂY BÂNU:	There's the question of this secret passage...
YÂMÂT:	I beg you, Ây Bânu...
ÂY BÂNU:	But I was bound by my promise to my anguished father on his deathbed

	to keep this secret even from you his cherished companion and my lifelong protector.
YÂMÂT:	What of it now, my Lady?
ÂY BÂNU:	Once the secret passage is known there's no resting at night without the fear of an ambush by roaming Tartars.
YÂMÂT:	*[Gazing intently at Ây Bânu]* We must think of that!
ÂY BÂNU:	I must be helped and obeyed before changing into a woman's habit. So be careful!
	[Hubbub outside.]
	What noise is this?
ATTENDANT:	*[Enters, panting]* Will there be an audience or Ây Bânu shall go to the roof of the palace?
YÂMÂT:	What for?
ATTENDANT:	Not having witnessed her arrival many do not believe in it.
YÂMÂT:	I smell a plot.
ÂY BÂNU:	Not I.
YÂMÂT:	You must take no risks.

ÂY BÂNU: What is to be, will be.

[Crowds clamouring and pressing against the door.]

ATTENDANT: By valiant Vatvât's leave
one of you may come in
on everyone's behalf.

[A man in a long black robe forces his way in.]

Who are you
in such a haste?
Unveil your face!
only one!

YÂMÂT: *[Stunned by his sight]*
Now, this is but a dead man
out of his grave.
I know him.
Tuy Khân!

ATTENDANT: *[Shocked]*
This cannot be!

YÂMÂT: On my soul, I swear!

ATTENDANT: Do graves throw up their dead?

YÂMÂT: The six Tuy Khâns you fashioned,
Ây Bânu
have conspired
to give their blood to the seventh
who now stands before you.
And there's no hope for me
anymore.

ATTENDANT: *[Gazing at newcomer]*
Yours must be a strange story.
In your place
I would not have revealed myself.

TUY KHÂN: *[To Attendant]*
Go out and stay out
until I call you in!

[To Yâmât.]

Both of you!

[Attendant hesitates.]

Didn't you hear me?

[Yâmât looks at Ây Bânu.]

ÂY BÂNU: *[To Yâmât and Attendant]*
Give a hand to Commander Oyerât
and see that those who cause unrest
whether Tuqânian
or TuyKhânian
are Subdued!

YÂMÂT: You shall be obeyed, Ây Bânu!

ATTENDANT: By your leave!

[Both exit.]

TUY KHÂN: They obey your command!

ÂY BÂNU: Welcome, Tuy Khân!
We Kalâtians salute one another
when we meet!

[Suldus pushes Jailer and Executioner on stage. They fall and stay prostrate on the ground.]

SULDUS: An absurd fantasy, Ây Bânu!
This foolish wretch
would have me believe
that the Seven-Headed Tuy Khân
is alive!

ÂY BÂNU: *[Continuing to look Tuy Khân in the eye]*
Is that so?

EXECUTIONER: *[Weeping]*
I swear!

JAILER: *[Weeping]*
By the light of my eyes
I swear!

SULDUS: What man is this?

[Vatvât, also terrified, has entered. Suldus walks backwards.]

Tuy Khân... indeed!

EXECUTIONER: Woe is me!
There's no hope for my life anymore.
In whom could I now
confide my grief?

JAILER: Of whom should I now
ask forgiveness?

TUY KHÂN: They shall both die!

ÂY BÂNU: You are both forgiven!

TUY KHÂN: *[Stunned]*

	Would you outbid me?
ÂY BÂNU:	This is Kalât, Tuy Khân as it was before you raped it. Now no more bloodshed!

[To Executioner and Jailer.]

Get up and go, men!

[The two, half dead, get up and bow.]

JAILER:	Tuy Khân be praised!
EXECUTIONER:	And Ây Bânu too!

[They dash out.]

TUY KHÂN:	*[Quickly to Suldus and Vatvât, who now approach him]* Stay outside until I call you!

[Hesitantly, they both look at Ây Bânu.]

ÂY BÂNU:	Indeed have this Firmân proclaimed throughout the city: "The armies of Tuy Khân "and Tuqâi Khân "shall unite! "Those who have stayed "are now defenders of Kalât. "They should both be given equal rations. "Whoever stays

	"shall have a piece of land to cultivate "and he who chooses to go "will be given a horse to ride "in exchange for his sword and armour!"
TUY KHÂN:	*[Furious, stamping the ground]* Begone both of you!
VATVÂT:	By your leave, Ây Bânu.

[Exit Vatvât and Suldus]

ÂY BÂNU:	Your shouts have grown louder, Tuy Khân since I saw you last.
TUY KHÂN:	You'll hear louder shouts from me, yet. Why have you put on my garb?
ÂY BÂNU:	You wore my dress the other day, remember!
TUY KHÂN:	I despised that cursed woman's dress!
ÂY BÂNU:	Not as much as I despise your garb.
TUY KHÂN:	Revenge belonged to me and you stole it from me. Who gave you the right to avenge my disgrace?
ÂY BÂNU:	Who told you that I avenged your disgrace? The seven-headed monster that you are you deserved your disgrace. Put your mind at rest. It was my own degradation that I avenged.

TUY KHÂN: What loathsome insolence is this?

ÂY BÂNU: Is it not degrading that a man
—a vile and depraved man at that—
should be treated as a woman
and a knave and a worthless
treacherous fool
should be clothed in a woman's garb?
They didn't
in truth
insult *you*, Tuy Khân
they unquestionably degraded *me*!
You're not a woman, man
but a vulgar
self-centered
inward-looking freak!
You don't give to the world
you only take from it.
Every woman in Kalât shall witness
that you are the monster
who has dipped both his hairy hands
in the blood of
at least one of her loved ones.

TUY KHÂN: Did I escape that abominable moat of misery
to come here
and put up with your foolish foibles?
Why, I lay with decaying corpses
in fetid water
And held out under the avalanche of dirt
poured into the moat
by a howling mob.
And in the darkness of night

>   I crawled out of that putrid hole
>   shivering with fever
>   in the wet, rancid garb of a dead man
>   and I was thankful
>   to find refuge
>   in a revolting lair of rats.
>   Why?
>   How could I endure all that misery
>   and yet
>   remain intact?
>   Because I was sustained
>   by my loathing for Tuqâi
>   and my lust for his blood.
>   I was hoarding hatred
>   to forge my weapon
>   for revenge.
>   Is it now possible
>   to let people say
>   that a woman snatched
>   my revenge?

ÂY BÂNU: So, *that's* the reason for your complaint!
You're raving
because I'm a woman!
But when
painted like a whore
you were carted around in abject disgrace
you didn't seem to complain!
In your place
I would've hanged myself!

TUY KHÂN: Fate had assigned him
to be my prey
so that I could thrust my claws

| | into his bowels
rip up his liver
sink my teeth into his heart
chew his gullet at leisure
and brandish his head
impaled on a pike.
You robbed me of my joy! |
|---|---|
| ÂY BÂNU: | You had died Tuy Khân
a miserable death
don't you remember?
And your death had been certified.
How could a dead man
clamour for revenge
or indulge in merriment! |
| TUY KHÂN: | Give me Tuqâi's corpse
and I shall have it slain
over and over again. |
| ÂY BÂNU: | While you did your best
to grow a beard in hiding
I
wisely
gathered an army
and went to war at once. |
| TUY KHÂN: | But how did my Commanders
obey a woman? |
| ÂY BÂNU: | Hadn't they already obeyed
a fake resemblance of a woman? |
| TUY KHÂN: | An impossible arrangement, that! |
| ÂY BÂNU: | They put up their best fight
did they not? |

TUY KHÂN:	On what promise?
ÂY BÂNU:	You were dead
and I was free.
Other than the prospect of captivity
and disgrace
what was your bequest to me?
I put to use the only possession I had.
My being.
And now
I have Kalât...
and its people
who sing their joy.
TUY KHÂN:	In praise of Ây Bânu
I know of other songs too
commissioned by Tuqâi
the hated Captive-Killer.
ÂY BÂNU:	Unlike you
he had a love of songs!
TUY KHÂN:	Damn his love of songs!
ÂY BÂNU:	Now, when did I hear the last one?
TUY KHÂN:	A son of a whore he was!
ÂY BÂNU:	You were captured by him
not I.
I captured him!
You lost Kalât
I salvaged it.
Death
like a hawk
circled over our heads
and followed us everywhere.

You weren't there
to see the sky
darkened with flags and pendants
and filled with dust.
you were instead
living it out in your rat-hole
growing a beard
doing... nothing!
And now, you've come
to share in victory.

TUY KHÂN: Not share in it
no!
The whole of victory is mine!
For I am the living Tuy Khân
and belong to the conquering race
in whose dominions
the sun rises and sets
at the same time.
The confirmation of my conquest
is on its way.
So is the decree of my governance.
Soon, messengers will be dispatched
to Soqdiân and Kâshqar
Khatâ and Khazar
Qandahâr, Urganj and Farqâneh.
The name "Tuy Khân"
shall top the crowns of ten Gates.
My disgrace will be forgotten
when I avenge myself on Kalâtians.
I am not called
The Seven-Headed Tuy Khân
for nothing!

All around these walls
I shall hang heads of Alâns
men and women
who laughed at me
in my misery.
I shall abolish
the custom of laughter
in this world!
Ohoy, where are you?
Robe-Master
attendant!

ÂY BÂNU: You move too fast, Tuy Khân.

TUY KHÂN: Patience be damned!
I swear
by the raging God of mountains
who has the world at His heels
that I shall presently break
the bones of Kalâtians
under my heel!

ÂY BÂNU: I swear
by the tears of the gentle Goddess
who reigns over the waters of the world
that you shall drown
in the milk
given by Kalâtian mothers
to their babes!

TUY KHÂN: No babes will be left in Kalât!

ÂY BÂNU: No Tuqâis
or Tuy Khâns
will be left in this world.
Only Kalât shall abide

	forever.
TUY KHÂN:	I shall lay it waste
from battlement to battlement.
Not a single wall
nor a lone tower
shall remain intact!
ÂY BÂNU:	Like an owl
make your roost in ruins!
For that is where you belong.
TUY KHÂN:	I've heard these words before
But where?
... Hah, there was a woman with five heads.
Away with fear!
Open the armoury!
Now for a clarion
to rouse my warriors
and bid them not to leave
a single Kalâtian alive!
ÂY BÂNU:	I did not recover Kalât
to hand it over
to an executioner.
Were it not for Ây Bânu
you'd still be crouching
in your lair
waiting for your beard to grow.
Don't forget that!
TUY KHÂN:	You treacherous shrew
go and replace that armour
with a woman's habit, at once!
It was the name of a man

	my name that set the seal on your victory for you're a mere woman —don't forget that!
ÂY BÂNU:	Have you nothing more to say?
TUY KHÂN:	Go to the Shabestân and change your garb! For women are better suited to men's bedchambers. Hold your insolent gaze! Stop countering my words and trying to raise yourself to my level! Obey me! A woman is no match for a man.
	[He goes out.]
ÂY BÂNU:	Well, Tuy Khân now that I cannot be your equal unless I shed as much blood as you stay and behold then! I will do what must be done. I will be a match to you, Tuy Khân… Ohoy, come… Commanders Valiant knights… Where are you?
	[Enter Suldus and Vatvât. Ây Bânu begins to take off pieces of armour one by one.]
ÂY BÂNU:	Well Commanders

	I must now remove my armour
for my bedchamber
is already being illuminated.
To prove the boundlessness of my affection
I stand by my pledge.
But between me
and the fulfillment of my promise
stands a monster
who wasn't there
when it was given.
Thus, while he lives
I cannot abide by my promise.
SULDUS:	Just as I thought!
VATVÂT:	This has rankled in me too.
SULDUS:	*[Feeling for his sword]*
But there is a way!
ÂY BÂNU:	I cannot conceive of any.
So I'll say nothing.
VATVÂT:	*[Draws his sword]*
A hint is all a man needs.
Now, away!
	[Swords drawn, they exit.]
ÂY BÂNU:	Fetch my mourning habit!
	[Old Alân women, ululating joyfully, enter.]

My dress of mourning! |
| OLD WOMAN 1: | Happy days to you Ây Bânu! |

	Kalât is beside itself with joy.
	Why this untimely woe?
ÂY BÂNU:	You never know.
	There's always some news on the way!

[Enter Pishmargs.]

OLD PISHMARG:	The last mutinies are crushed
	and every defiant rebel
	has laid down his sword.
	The war has come to an end.
YOUNG PISHMARG:	Albeit, at a high cost.
	The valiant Oyerât
	died for your cause.
ÂY BÂNU:	Oyerât?
OLD PISHMARG:	He smiled at the arrow
	that pierced his manly frame
	and went on to fighting the end.
YOUNG PISHMARG:	So did Yâmât
	who made himself the target
	to many arrows.
ÂY BÂNU:	Bless your soul, Yâmât!
	May God forgive me!

[Robe-Master and Attendant enter with a black dress.]

YOUNG PISHMARG:	What's your command?
ÂY BÂNU:	Command?
OLD PISHMARG:	Kalât calls for you
	with a single voice

                    while waiting for your direction.
Townspeople have already begun
to illuminate the City
and exchange
felicities and favours
give alms
and offer sacrifices
dance
and make merry.

YOUNG PISHMARG: Yet, everywhere
there's a nagging fear
about Tuy Khân's return
from the Netherworld.

OLD PISHMARG: That usurper of other people's honors!

YOUNG PISHMARG: What's your command?

ÂY BÂNU: Let clarions bewail
the death of valiant Oyerât
and brave Yâmât.
Cover them both with flowers!
Sitting in ashes
for three days and nights
Ây Bânu shall mourn
the death of young Yâmât
who was an Alân.
Shackle the two Tartar Generals
Suldus and Vatvât
in the adjoining chambers
and have them publicly executed!

OLD PISHMARG: For what crime?

ÂY BÂNU: For murdering my ill-starred husband,

> Tuy Khân
> who escaped the sword of his enemy
> only to be slain
> by that of his friends.

OLD PISHMARG: What's the meaning of this, pray?

> *[Tuy Khân's head falls on the ground.]*
>
> But...
> Well...
> Let us not lose time.
> Come!
>
> *[Exit Alâns, with swords drawn. Women ululate.]*

ÂY BÂNU:
> *[Sits gently beside the head]*
> Well
> you showed me the way, Tuy Khân.
> Am I your equal, now?
>
> *[Gently rises.]*
>
> Let Alâns savour this victory
> and see for themselves
> that Mongols, too
> can be broken!
> Let two messengers be swiftly dispatched
> to the two Arâns:
> one set in the heart of the salt desert
> beside the City of Kâssiân
> the other
> Arân of Azarân
> refreshed by the waters

of the untarnished lake of Vân.

[A man quickly goes out.]

Help me now
into my funeral robes!

[Old women, ululating, help her into the robes, which they have been holding ready. Attendant and Robe-Master cover Tuy's head with a piece of cloth and remove it. Women, wailing and praying. Young Pishmarg enters.]

YOUNG PISHMARG: Your bidding's done, Ây Bânu.
The two villainous Tartar Generals
are stitched together with arrows.
Birds have now returned to our skies.
Songsters sing this victory
with bells and cymbals.

ÂY BÂNU: Have this message put up
on all the Six Gates of the City.
"Kalât waits for her wounds to heal.
"Let those who have walked in rags
"and suffered hunger
"be clothed and fed.
"And the ones who have thrived on blood
"sheathe their daggers.
"No more revenge, no more!
"For death has had
"so long a life
"by snatching away
"so many lives from us."

*[Someone takes this message quickly away.
Old Pishmarg and Attendant enter.]*

ATTENDANT: Here comes the envoy of Tongqut Khân
bearing his Highness' Firmân
as well as his gifts.
Open the way
for the eminent ambassador
the interpreter of the Faqfur
and the confidant of the mighty Khân!

*[Envoy and his companion enter.
Alâns make way.]*

ENVOY: Weeks ago
as I was about to leave
the august presence
of the Supreme Potentate of our time
reports of varying natures
concerning the Fortress City of Kalât
continued to arrive.
His Highness
being unaware of the exact identity
of the Conqueror of the city
entrusted me with His dread Firmân
upon which
I was to set down in Oyquri letters
the renowned name of the said
conqueror
amidst the four seals of His Highness.
"Once the Firmân is delivered"
His Highness solemnly decreed that
"Tartar sallies on Kalât must cease".
He bade me then

	to set forth
	post haste.
	The light gait of my nimble mule, however
	was turned into a limp
	by the unfortunate roughness of the road.
	Now, it seems
	that I have arrived
	at the very end of the final battle.
	Be that as it may
	take me to the acclaimed Conqueror now
	—quick!

OLD PISHMARG: You stand before the Conqueror of Kalât!

ENVOY: A woman?

OLD PISHMARG: Ây Bânu!

ENVOY: I see
but cannot believe!
The mighty Tartar
on hearing this
would likely exclaim
"some woman!"
Come scribe,
set down the name!
Here's the pen-case
and the Firmân!
And now, Ây Bânu
the Conqueror of Kalât
and the holder of the Firmân of Governance!
As your name is being inscribed

| | in its rightful place
may I ask
if you have some word
or a message
that you would have me deliver
unto the great Tartar? |
|---|---|
| ÂY BÂNU: | Indeed I have.
Proclaim this message
throughout the realm:
"Let women bring into this world
"children
"filled with loathing for war.
"The world is ruined by heroes.
"It is for us to reclaim it." |

[All bow before her.]

| STORYTELLER: | Sing the song of joy and sorrow.
The world is a ruin
as far as the eye can see.
Hail to him
who reclaims.
Hail to him
who brings about
a better world. |
|---|---|

[Lights fade.]

www.ingramcontent.com/pod-product-compliance
Lightning Source LLC
Chambersburg PA
CBHW020527080526
44583CB00013B/765